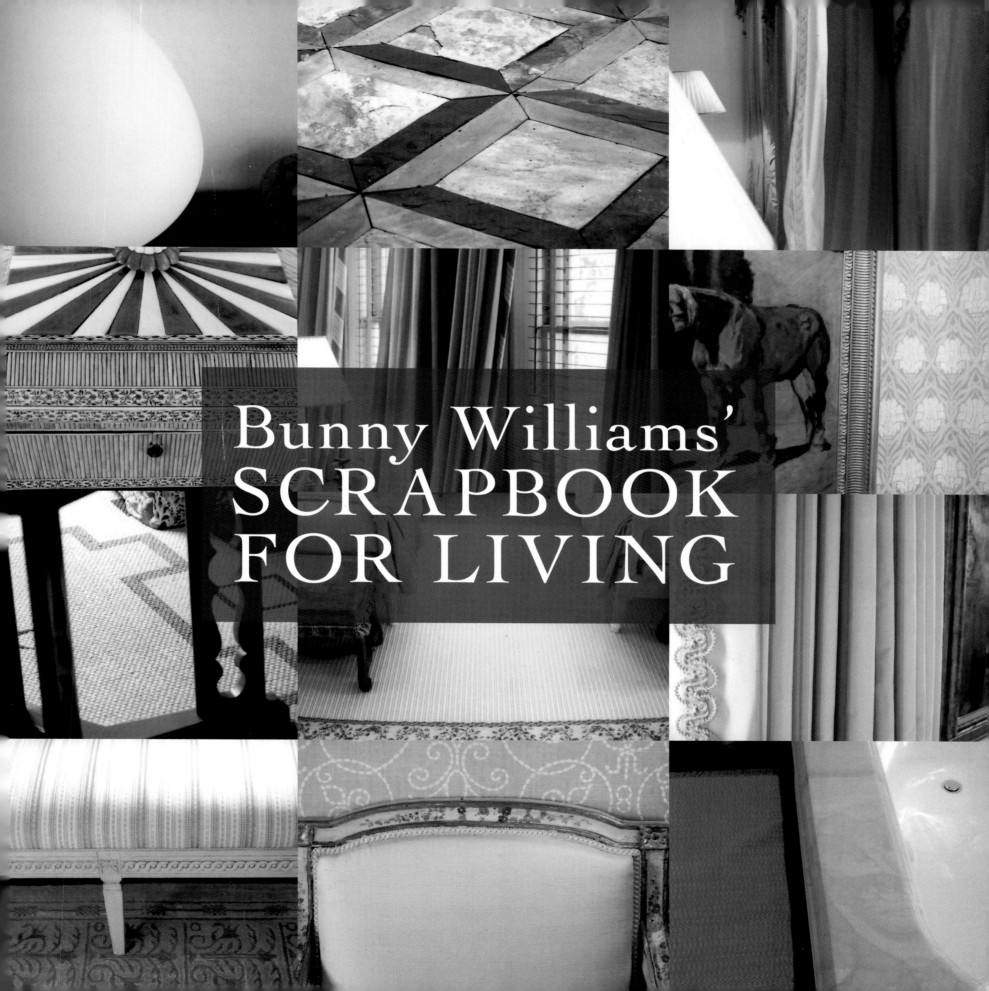

# Bunny Williams' SCRAPBOOK FOR LIVING

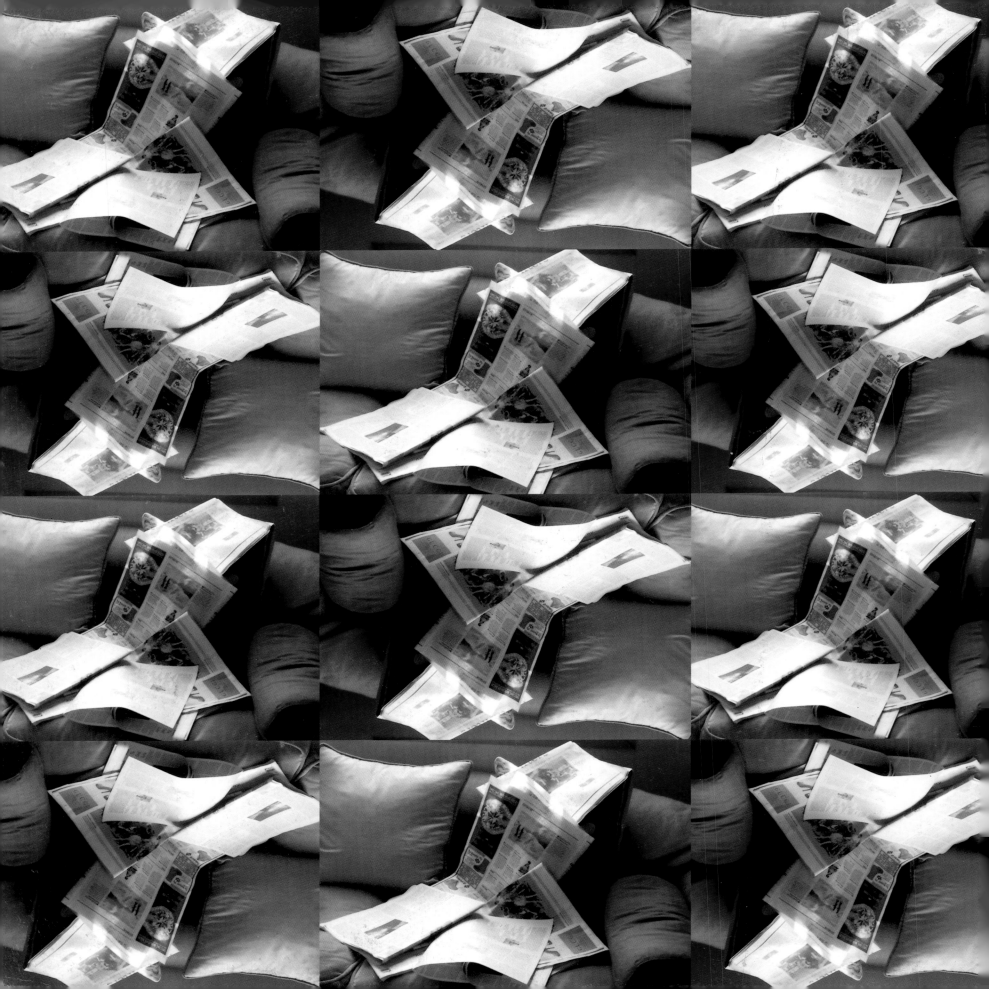

# Bunny Williams' SCRAPBOOK FOR LIVING

Place Portraits by Amy Archer

STEWART, TABORI & CHANG, NEW YORK

# { ACKNOWLEDGMENTS }

THIS BOOK WOULD NEVER HAVE COME to fruition without the help and support of many people. I offer my heartfelt thanks to Leslie Stoker, who encouraged me to do another book and held my hand along the way. To Amy Archer, whose vision and talent make the images in this book so unique. To Doug Turshen and David Huang, who somehow always seem to pull all of the elements together in the most amazing way. To Dervla Kelly, who gave my scribbles order and clarity.

To my friends and clients whose houses appear throughout the pages—Lee Link, Nancy Power, Tina Beebe, Buzz Yudell, Jane and Stephen Garmey, Betsy Smith, Leslie and Abbott Sprague, Marc and Cathy Lasry, Christel De Haan, Karen and Chris Watkins, and Steven and Cheri Friedman. I want you all to know how appreciative I am.

To Carolyn Coulter, my assistant, who put all my scraps in order.

And especially to John Rosselli, my patient and supportive partner.

—*Bunny Williams*

# { CONTENTS }

10 Introduction

CHAPTER I
14 Making Your Home Function
18 Mudrooms
22 Entrance Halls and Staircases
28 Living Rooms
40 Offices and Project Rooms
50 Playrooms
52 Dining Areas or Rooms
60 Libraries and Books
68 Lighting

CHAPTER II
72 Bringing a Home to Life
76 Flowers
84 Scents
88 Candlelight
90 Artwork
94 Fireplaces
98 Mirrors
102 Comfort

CHAPTER III
106 Keeping a House Organized
110 Laundry Rooms
112 Linen Closets
116 Clothes Closets
120 Pantry
124 China Closets
132 Useful Containers

CHAPTER IV

**138 Bedrooms and Bathrooms**

146 Making a Perfect Bed

150 Making a Bathroom Special

CHAPTER V

**154 Personal Touches**

158 Photographs

164 Living with Animals

170 Collections

CHAPTER VI

**176 Maintenance**

178 Housekeeping

CHAPTER VII

**182 Entertaining**

188 Planning Parties

192 Cocktail Parties

194 Seated Dinners

196 Buffets

198 Necessities to Have on Hand

204 Setting the Table

208 Bar

210 Menus

214 Recipes

CHAPTER VIII

**216 Making Your Own Scrapbook**

218 Inspirations

220 Favorite Books

222 Resources

# { INTRODUCTION }

What is it that gives a home real magic? A home that, from the moment you walk through the door, creates an impression of not just beauty, but of emotion as well; a home with a soul. A place that is welcoming, accessible, and completely alluring; one that is filled with signs of life: books, flowers, a desk cluttered with mail. Over the years, I have had the opportunity to be a guest in many, many homes, from tiny cottages to palatial estates, but the ones I remember the most are the homes in which the owners lived not only with great style but also with a real sense of what a home is all about. The ones I remember are those that made me feel incredibly comfortable. The smell of tuberoses wafting through the room; a bench in front of a warm fireplace piled high with magazines I could not wait to read, and a comfortable chair just begging me to curl up in it; glistening silver picture frames filled with smiling faces on a large table in front of a sunny window; rooms filled with furniture, no matter what the style, arranged for conversation. Comfortable chairs surrounding a dining table and the smell of baking brownies floating from the kitchen; platters waltzing across the buffet, waiting for the roast chicken; shelves in the kitchen filled with marvelous pottery bowls and pitchers all beautifully arranged. Despite the comfort in these houses, great care is also taken: Furniture is dusted and polished; glass and mirrors sparkle.

On thinking about the magic of these houses, I decided I wanted to write another book. I considered calling it *Life After Decorating,* but I thought that might sound as though I had experienced an epiphany, abandoned my career, and taken a whole new direction in life. Instead, what I want to explore in this book are the details that I have found in these homes that transcended decorating and became something more.

So I came up with the title *Scrapbook for Living,* and when my dear friend Betsy Smith introduced me to the work of artist Amy Archer, I knew I had found a photographer who could capture the ethereal feeling that real homes radiate. Amy's "place portraits" capture the details of a room in a completely unique way. She set off to photograph not only my home in the Dominican Republic, but also some of my clients' homes and the homes of some of my friends—all people who live with great personal style and panache—where I have been welcomed many times and love going.

Lee and Fritz Link's chalet-style house overlooking a valley in Connecticut is filled with art collected over the years, and there are books everywhere, even set between the spindles of a staircase leading up to a heavenly loft space. Nancy Power, a fabulous landscape designer, lives in a modern house painted the most amazing colors in Santa Monica. The interior of the house opens to the outside, where the outdoor living space, an exciting and exuberant garden, is an extension of the house. Jane and Stephen Garmey—Jane is a writer and Stephen is a retired Episcopal priest, artist, and Russian scholar—live in an eighteenth-century clapboard house filled with treasures from their many travels, arranged in the most artistic way.

All of my friends are great cooks and entertain beautifully. Nancy thinks nothing of having sixteen people for dinner in a relatively small space, because she is equipped with all the china, glasses, and napkins that she needs and knows how to make simple yet delicious meals. Jane is a great cook (she has even written a cookbook), so we love to join them around their large stone table, usually set for twelve. Everyone sits close together, sharing tasty meals and animated conversation.

What I want to do through the ideas and details within the pages of this book is to enable you to take hold of your homes and make them welcoming to all who enter. Today, our lives are over-programmed with careers, children, activities, and charity work, and the moments we have to nurture our homes are few and far between. That is why it is so important to organize your home to fit your needs, from arranging the furniture to cleaning your closets, from having the right container for a quick flower arrangement to keeping a perfectly stocked pantry, from planning a table setting to making a welcoming bed. From the front door to the basement, I want to share my scrapbook of ideas for making a home not only functional but a beautiful, welcoming paradise that you, your family, and your friends will never want to leave.

{ CHAPTER I }

# Making Your Home Function

T HE PLANNING OF ANY HOME SHOULD begin with function first, then design. Whether you have one room or many, thought has to be given to how the room or rooms will be used. From the front door to the back, each space has a purpose, and one has to provide the necessary plan for its function. Every detail must be considered: Where will the wet umbrellas go? Where do the coats find a home? The smaller the space, the more we have to plan, as we may not have the luxury of many rooms that can be used for different purposes. One room may have to function for entertaining, working, or watching television, but if thought is given to its use, a beautiful space can be created. A large table can function for dining as well as a desk area.

One of the most important things to think about and provide is storage. Whether it is the kitchen, living room, or bedroom, there must be places to put away our "things." Otherwise we will never be able to have order, and a room without order will never be attractive. We often do not have enough closet space. It is important to select pieces of furniture that can hold your files, papers, china, wrapping paper—whatever it is that needs to be tucked away and have a place of its own.

Try to find space in your home that can be used for projects so that everything can be left out until there is spare time to get back to the work. Find an area that becomes the pets' special place, a spot they like to go when you have to leave them alone for a time. A home is a place where every member of the family should feel welcome.

As we live year after year in our homes, one of the most important things to do is to constantly edit. Books and magazines, family pictures, mementos from trips, unused plates that remain from what was once a complete set—all these things multiply and need to be sorted through and in some cases given away. I am always giving books to the local library for their annual book sales. Donate objects and old clothes to a local charity for a tag sale. Try to keep your possessions under control. It will make it much easier to keep your house in order.

# { MUDROOMS }

I FIND THAT OFTEN THE SERVICE ENTRANCE or back door gets used more than the front entrance. This entrance is usually near the garage or parking, so it provides the most convenient access to a house. This is why it should be special; a lot of thought and planning needs to go into this space to make it as inviting as the front hall. Thought has to be given to the practical as well as aesthetic side. Stone or tile floors are impervious to rain and mud. A practical rug that is easy to clean will serve a valuable purpose.

Think of where you'll put coats, wet umbrellas, dog leashes, and other items brought into the house. Sports equipment needs to have a place to go other than the middle of the floor. If a space is planned and designed for your things, then there will be complete harmony between aesthetics and practicality. For the most-used entrances, I suggest including not only closets but also pegs for coats, hats, and scarves. People are always in a hurry and often do not take the time to hang things in the closet. Chairs and benches are needed not only for putting on boots, but also as a place for packages before they are dispensed through the house. Cubbies are great for sports equipment, and if each child has his or her own, things do not get mixed up. Mirrors are important, as we have to see how we look coming and going.

A wall with pegs makes hanging up coats and hats quick and easy; they are also handy for leashes and bags.

A bench is a great place to change into boots and then store shoes underneath.

Always find a spot for a mirror.

A pile rug makes a great mat that prevents the tracking of dirt through the house. Use as large a rug as possible. Old Oriental carpets are very forgiving, as is any kind of rug with a pattern.

A chest of drawers provides a home for gloves, scarves, and keys.

Keep a supply of canvas shopping bags in a closet or hung on pegs. They come in handy for carrying everything from clothes for the cleaners to gifts, toys, and other things we always seem to be taking from place to place. I especially love ones from L.L. Bean.

# { ENTRANCE HALLS AND STAIRCASES }

THE ENTRANCE HALL IS THE FIRST IMPRESSION guests have of your home when they step through the front door. Opening the door to wonderful scents and a beautifully organized space will have lasting impact. If your family comes in and out of the front door many times during the course of the day, it's also important to provide easy-access storage for coats, umbrellas, scarves, canvas shopping bags, etc. So this space must not only be smashing but very well thought out.

As an entrance hall has open floor space, it is the ideal place to have a special floor finish or showcase a drop-dead rug. Wooden floors can be painted in a favorite design or stenciled to resemble a marquetry pattern.

Paint the interior of a coat closet an exciting color
for a nice surprise when you hang up coats.

Use matching wooden hangers in the front hall closet;
hang a scented sachet to give a delicious aroma to your coats.

A chest of drawers provides a great storage piece in a hall.

Always hang as large a mirror as possible over a chest or table.

The front hall table is the perfect place for flower arrangements or flowering plants. Tuck a favorite scented candle nearby for added ambience.

Make sure there are chairs or benches to be used as a perch for removing boots or resting a bag.

A large Chinese cylinder vase can be used as an attractive umbrella stand.

Stairs can have carpet runners with three-inch borders on each side for safety. If the stairs are left bare, do not wax the steps, as they will be very slippery.

Stone floors with a honed finish are much safer and less slippery than a highly polished floor. I also feel that the honed surface has a warmer feeling than the high glossy shine of an over-polished floor.

Use a tapestry or large painting on a stairway wall for dramatic effect.

A great collection of prints can also be interesting when winding up the wall of a staircase.

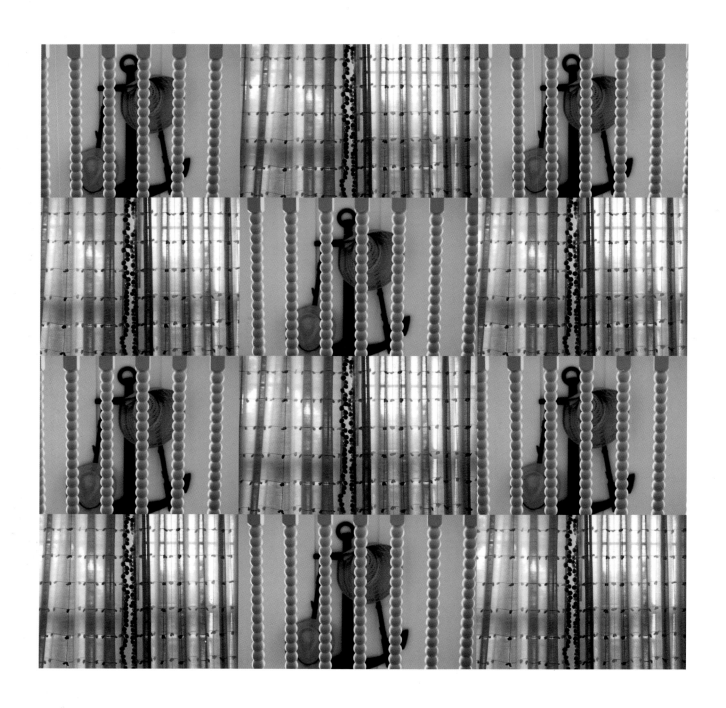

# { LIVING ROOMS }

THE HEART OF EVERY HOME USED TO BE THE LIVING ROOM, but since many homes today have a "family room" or "great room" off the kitchen, the living room often gets abandoned. Usually when a client says to me, "We never use this room," I survey the room and see that very little thought has been given to making it a living space. Not only must furniture be placed in such a way that there are comfortable seating areas where people can group around a coffee table (perhaps with a plate of delicious tid-bits), but there should be a place to put a laptop, play a game of cards, or do a jigsaw puzzle. The room needs to be inviting for a single person, a small family gathering, or a large party.

Sometimes I go into a room that is beautifully furnished but has no soul. There are no personal mementos, family photographs, objects found on a trip, no books, no flowers, no feeling that there is a favorite chair used for reading the paper. I get the feeling I am in a grand hotel lobby. But when you walk into a living room with flowers on the tabletops, a delicious scent filling the air, a cashmere throw over the back of a comfortable chair, books piled among family photographs, soft full pillows to sink into on an inviting sofa, a silver tray filled with bottles, glasses, and an ice bucket nearby . . . well, then you feel the warmth as well as the style.

Arrange furniture for conversation.
Chairs and sofas should relate to each other, forming an area where six to eight people
can be near enough to create an intimate group.

Small tables are a must. Make sure that each person
has one near him or her for a drink.

Include different types of chairs in a group.
Not everyone can get out of a deep sofa or chair, so a comfortable but
straight or open armchair should be in every group.

Deep sofas should have lots of big pillows across the back to adjust the depth.

**Check the seat height** of chairs when placing them in a group. It is unpleasant to be sitting in a chair with a high seat (eighteen or nineteen inches) next to someone in a low seat.

**Chairs with higher seats** should be shallow; lower-seated chairs can be much deeper.

**Place a bench under tables** or in front of a fireplace for extra seating when needed.

**A low coffee table** or upholstered ottoman should be placed in the middle of the group. This provides a surface to hold books, magazines, a plate of hors d'oeuvres, a bowl of nuts, or even a small bouquet of flowers.

# { OFFICES AND PROJECT ROOMS }

I F THERE IS ONE SPACE IN A HOUSE that I really cannot do without, it is a home office/project room where I can work, create, and be completely content. This is a place that no one else ever has to see, but it holds everything I need: my computer, reference books, magazines, paints and papers, wrapping papers, sewing machine, knitting and needlepoint projects (in case I have a spare moment), and a gift closet.

Find spaces in your home that can be used for projects. My mother turned the attic of the house I grew up in into a great combination playroom/project room. There were long tables set up where she could work on her decorations that would be sold at the church Christmas bazaar and I could do art projects. There was a sewing machine always ready and drawers filled with scissors, glues, wonderful glittery paper, sequins, and ribbons all ready to become sparkly Christmas ornaments. Off to the side of this long space was an alcove that held old trunks with my "dress-up" clothes. This is where I put on what I am sure were dreadful plays with my friends. There were always princesses, witches, and fortune tellers in each play, which made for very creative costumes and make-up. Whether it is for children, a husband, or a family memeber who works at home, everyone should have a space they feel is theirs.

Working or project areas can be created in a basement, attic, small spare room, or even a closet, but there is nothing better than having everything you want nearby with space to keep it.

**A desk can be made** from ready-made file drawers from an office supply company and a wood top that is as long as possible. Several file cabinets can be placed together to create pedestals on each side of an opening. One side might have file drawers, the other shallow drawers for paper and supplies. Above this can be cabinets to store paper, wrapping paper, paints, books, etc. The long desk area can hold a fax/printer/scanner and computer. I often scan pictures or recipes that interest me from books or magazines and put them in my scrapbook.

**If space allows,** a tall island in the middle of a room is perfect for painting, drawing, sewing, and wrapping packages. Counter-height stools work well around an island. I find I do everything but deskwork here, as I have a big surface to spread out on. And John likes to paint, so the island gives him a place to work in the room as well.

**Flat, deep file cabinets** with narrow drawers are fantastic if you have the space. Though typically designed for architectural plans, they make fabulous storage for wrapping paper, tapes, cards, and sewing necessities, and because they are tall, they double as a perfect work counter.

## If there is a closet

in the room, it should be fitted with shelves. Shelves can hold containers loaded with supplies for any project one wants to do. Also, I always like to have a gift closet. I learned this from my mother. Whenever I travel or am in a shop and see something really special—maybe on sale—I purchase the item and put it away. This way, I have a small token to take for a dinner host, birthday, or housewarming gift and do not have to scurry around at the last minute and, in desperation, settle on something I then pay too much for.

## Some hints about giving gifts (from a person

who has received many): Don't try to give an object that you think is perfect for someone's home. Very few people really understand what someone else will like. That fabulous object that you thought your friend would adore may end up in a closet, not because it wasn't fabulous, but because it just was not to her taste. Unless you know the recipient really well, give things that are practical, like a box of candles, a set of white napkins, or a delicious box of cookies or chocolates.

# { PLAYROOMS }

I T IS ALWAYS AMAZING TO ME that the younger a person the more things they have. Toys, games, stuffed animals, and Nintendo games seem to multiply overnight. Large straw hampers or baskets that fit under a coffee table offer great storage and allow easy access at playtime. Low shelves placed around a room or under a window are ideal spots for board games and books, and small children can reach them easily. No matter where children play, the most important consideration is how to tidy up the space quickly after what can look like a major storm has gone through the room. Having plenty of attractive hampers, trunks, and shelves will make light work of cleaning up the aftermath.

For teenagers, an attic or basement can become a perfect clubhouse at home with the addition of a Ping-Pong or billiard table, a card table, a large TV, and plenty of casual seating. When provided with a refrigerator full of drinks and a cabinet of snacks, teenagers will never want to leave. When I was growing up in Virginia, my parents did just that, turning over the basement to us. My mother felt more comfortable when she knew where we were, and my friends loved coming over to our house.

I love doing jigsaw puzzles and playing gin rummy, so a card table is a must for me. This can be tucked into the corner of a living room, playroom, or library. If you have a forty-eight-inch or fifty-four-inch top that can be put over the top of the card table, then it can also be used for dinner.

# { DINING AREAS OR ROOMS }

**M**EALS ARE SOME OF THE MOST IMPORTANT MOMENTS we have as a family. We need to make time for our family and friends, and gathering over lunch, dinner, or breakfast is a perfect time. The most important thing is to plan where you will eat and how to make the meal easy to serve.

I love eating in different places in our house. We have small informal dinners in the kitchen. Larger meals are eaten in the dining room or at a large stone table in our conservatory. In our apartment in New York, where I turned the dining room into a library, we eat at a table that also functions as my worktable. I use trays from the kitchen—with place mats, napkins, glasses, silverware, and dinner plates—which we can easily take back and forth. What is important is that you have a table that is comfortable for dining—be it round or rectangular—and a surface nearby on which to serve the food. This way the food can be set out and everyone can help themselves.

Dining tables are best when they can be flexible to accommodate various numbers of people. A fifty-four- or sixty-inch round table can seat up to eight people or if it can be extended with a leaf in the middle, can hold up to twelve. Recently, for a large rectangular room, I designed a dining table made up of three fifty-four-inch square tables which, when placed together, can sit sixteen people. The table can be separated and the dining room can hold twenty-four people. For a small group, one of the square tables can be set alone and seat six or eight people. Tables that have flexibility will make it easy to accommodate various numbers of family or friends.

No matter where you eat, make sure there is a generous side table or long cabinet for the buffet. A cabinet also provides great storage for dishes, silver, place mats, or other things needed for setting the table.

if you make an effort to get everyone together at the table, it will become a habit and a time you will all look forward to. Turn off the television and iPhones and have a conversation.

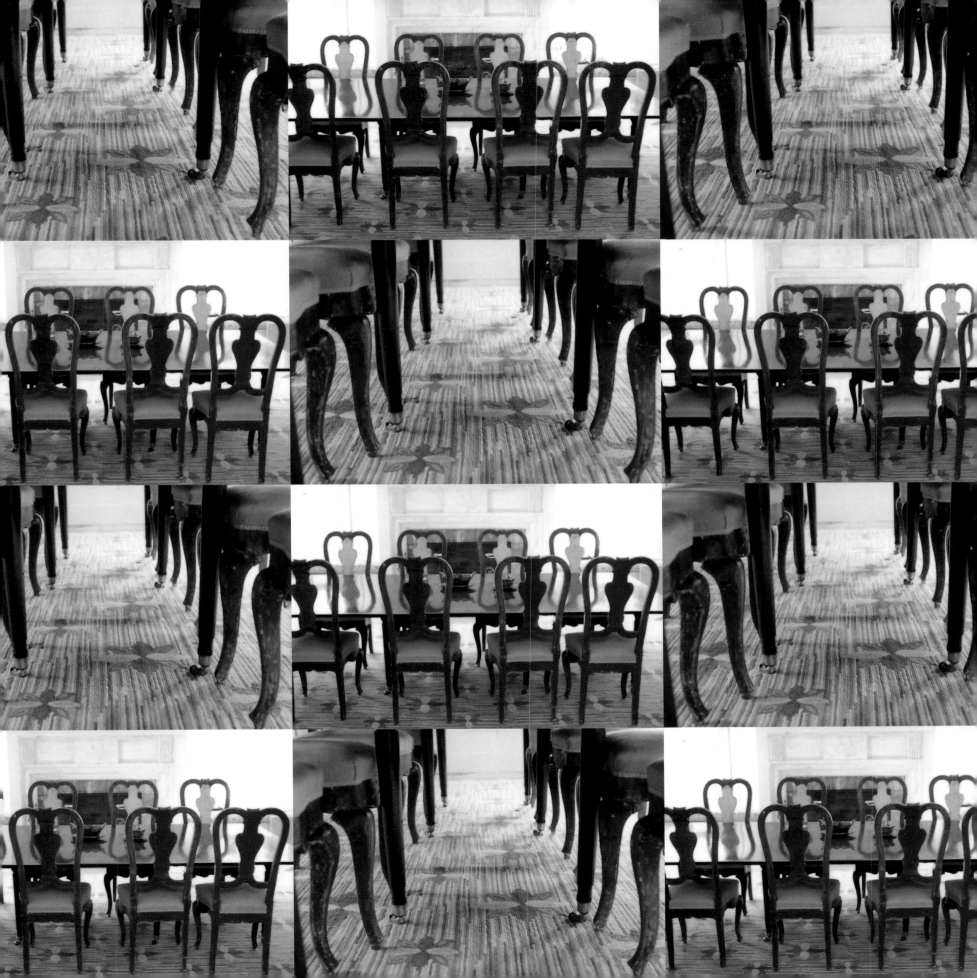

**Dining chairs do not have to match.** It is often helpful to have two sets of chairs—one set around the table and another set throughout the house, in halls or bedrooms, that can be put into use for a large event.

**Formal dining rooms** look better with a set of chairs, especially if there is a long table. A different style of chair, such as one with an upholstered back, can be used at each end of the table for variation.

**When choosing dining room furniture,** try to find chairs that are a different color than the table. If the table is wood, painted or lacquer chairs make a wonderful contrast and a more interesting combination than wood chairs. A stone table can have wooden chairs or upholstered chairs around it.

**Lighting is so, so important** in a dining room. If the room has an overhead chandelier, it must be on a dimmer. Light from sconces on the wall or from lamps on a side table can supplement the overhead lighting. I have been in too many dining rooms with too much light, which completely destroys any atmosphere or romance. It is better to have less light than more.

For dinners, lower the light from electric sources and use candles. You can never have too many candles. Votives on the table provide flattering low light. Candlesticks with simple glass hurricane shades add ambience on a side table or mantel.

It is important to consider sound in a dining room, since there are often many people talking. If the floor is bare, upholstered chairs help in softening the sound. If you find a room too noisy, add a rug.

If you set trays in the kitchen, it is easy to take them to any table in your home, and eating in different spaces is fun.

# { LIBRARIES AND BOOKS }

WHENEVER I GO INTO A HOME FILLED WITH FABULOUS BOOKS, I know that I am going to have interesting conversations with the owner. For those of us who collect books, there just never seem to be enough shelves to hold all the volumes we amass over the years. Hallways are often unused spaces and can hold narrow bookcases. A nook with built-in shelves, a comfortable chair, and a reading light nearby makes a marvelous place to curl up with the latest mystery.

The most difficult thing is to keep books organized so you can find a specific one when you want it.

## Group books by subject. Garden books should be placed together, as should cookbooks, novels, and books on art, design, etc.

## Stack books on the floor, putting all the books of one size in a pile. When you put the books on the shelves, place other books horizontally on top if there is room. This way you can get more books on a shelf.

## Placing objects in between rows of books provides an added dimension. It is also interesting to lay some books flat in a low stack with a small object set on top.

**It is important** to get enough light on books so that you can read their titles. Adding sconces to the divisions between shelves will provide great light. Long light fixtures especially designed for bookcases can be added to the top of a row of shelves.

**Put good novels,** mysteries, and biographies that you have read in guest rooms. I often put out current paperbacks, which guests are welcome to take if they are in the middle of reading them.

**Put current picture books** on tables or benches in the living room so guests will feel free to thumb through them while relaxing.

**Edit! Give away the books** you have read and don't want to keep or those you will never read. If you don't, there will be no end to your collection.

# { LIGHTING }

THE LIGHTING IN ANY ROOM CREATES A STRONG IMPRESSION. Lighting must come from several sources in a room, and overhead lights must be controlled by dimmer switches. After all, sometimes we want to create a mood, and other times we need all the light we can get.

In a large room, the light from the ceiling can come from several sources. A decorative light fixture in the center of a room can be supplemented by architectural lights installed in the ceiling that wash the exterior walls. In a low-ceilinged space, use flat fixtures that hang closer to the ceiling; in taller rooms, hang chandeliers to add interest.

Sconces against the wall add light at eye level and cut the unpleasant glare that can come when the only light source is from the ceiling. I like the bulbs on sconces to have shades to diffuse the light. Sconces can also be mounted on bookcases and in stairwells—places where light is needed. For staircases that have more than one floor, lanterns can be linked together, one on top of the other, with a decorative chain so that each landing receives the correct amount of light.

I love interesting lampshades. In a modern room, all the shades (the few that there are) should be the same. In a more eclectic space, you can have fun with patterned fabrics that look nice with the lamps in the room.

{ CHAPTER II }

# Bringing a Home to Life

O NE WAY I LIKE TO REALLY RELAX IS TO
come home, turn on the music—it may be Beethoven or Maria Callas, Diana Krall or Smokey Robinson, depending on my mood—and just spend time nurturing my house, reorganizing books, moving objects around, arranging the bunch of pale cream roses that I bought at the corner market on my way home from work. A house needs attention just like the children, a husband, and the family pet do. Does the large upholstered chair need a pillow? Is the furniture in the correct place? Are the pillows fluffed up? Did I leave out the day's newspaper for John to read? Are the current issues of magazines on the coffee table?

It is important to find time to really look at your rooms. Sit down alone and really take in every detail. Are you bored with the way things look? Could new art, rearranging, and editing what you have give your rooms a facelift?

Whenever I go into a room we are going to use, I always make sure it seems alive. In the winter, I light the fire or a scented candle and adjust the lights. In the summer, I open the French doors so we can feel the warm breeze. I light the candle in the hurricane lamp on the coffee table and make sure there is ice in the bucket on the drinks tray. Then I feel the room come to life.

# { FLOWERS }

HOMES REALLY ARE LIKE PEOPLE. If it is not groomed or brought to life with flowers, plants, fires, music, candlelight, or pleasant scents, a house can seem forlorn and sad. It may be perfectly decorated, but without these warm touches it can appear lifeless. Having the right containers for plants and flowers stored away in a closet is a good place to start. I always have a variety of cachepots ready to receive a plant from the greenhouse or the grocery store. Something in bloom—paperwhites, orchids, azaleas, primroses, or a beautiful fern—can be dropped into a waiting container and placed in the front hall or on a coffee table in the living room. My containers vary from china to wood to pottery to simple handwoven baskets. If the holder is porous, a liner is needed. This can be a plastic baggie or a plastic food container, but it is very important because you do not want water seeping out and leaving marks on furniture. I always keep a bag of Spanish moss to fill in around the top of the container to cover the pot. Different-size cachepots with interior measurements of four to ten inches will hold most standard plastic pots. Use cachepots with straight sides, or square ones. In the winter, when flowers are so much more expensive, I buy a lot of plants and the cachepots are frequently in use.

Have small containers on hand, such as silver julep cups, pitchers, and small glass vases. These look great filled with flowers with the stems cut short. Place them on an end table, in a powder room, or next to a bed.

Arrange flowers in shades of one color— reds and pinks—or close colors such as yellow and orange. These arrangements make more of an impact than a multicolored bouquet that may clash with the colors in the room. I always choose flowers that complement the palette of the room.

Keep blocks of Oasis floral foam or several pieces of chicken wire on hand in case you need to arrange flowers in larger containers. This will make flower arranging so much easier.

Bowls and flat plates look beautiful with a still life of luscious fruit. Try to find fruit with its leaves and stems still attached.

# { SCENTS }

N O MATTER HOW BEAUTIFUL A ROOM MAY BE, it will be a complete turn-off to a guest if it has a stale or musty scent. There is something very special about coming into a room that smells delicious. It is easy to get used to our surroundings and not notice how our house may smell to others. It is important first to make sure that rooms are clean. Open the windows often to bring in fresh air. Then you can add subtle scents from candles or, even easier, scented oils that come with sticks that emit fragrance continuously.

I prefer light, nonintrusive, fresh scents, with a flower base such as freesia or iris. They make it seem as though there is a flower bouquet somewhere in the room.

# Favorite candles

Treillage: Hedges

Diptyque: Figuier Vert, Jasmine, and Freesia

Nest: Bamboo

Rigaud: Cypress

Voluspa: Fleurs de Fete or Soleil


# Favorite oil-based scents

Antica Farmacista: Magnolia, Tuberose, Fig, and Magnolia

Agraria: Lemon Verbena, Jasmine, and Fig

# { CANDLELIGHT }

IF YOU HAVE EVER BEEN IN A ROOM TOTALLY LIT BY CANDLELIGHT, you will certainly remember the magic that the soft flickering light gave to the space. Today, we have lighting coming from everywhere: downlights, uplights, lamps. For practical purposes, we need a lot of light for reading or working. (I often wonder how Thomas Jefferson accomplished what he did with no electricity—writing the Declaration of Independence by candlelight. Amazing.) But for atmosphere, we need to reduce the electric wattage and add a few candles. In all my lamps, I try to have either two bulbs or a three-way bulb so I can have maximum brightness when I am working on a project or cut it in half for a dinner party.

A hurricane lamp (that is, a glass shade that protects a candle's flame) is a great way to create atmosphere, as it sparkles and enhances the light. Keep beautiful hurricanes on a coffee table or the mantel for easy access. Dim all light from the ceiling; there is nothing worse than too much overhead light, as it causes a glare and is harsh on the eyes and unflattering. Hurricane shades can be found in blue, green, amber, and red, as well as clear—all of which are really beautiful.

Votive candles are also a perfect way to add ambience. I am always looking for unusual votive candleholders, which I use not only when setting a table but also around the house in different places, such as mantels and side tables, to add a little sparkle.

# { ARTWORK }

AFTER MANY YEARS OF BEING A DESIGNER, I have become very aware of how important the addition of artwork of any type is to a room. I am always excited to work with clients who have artwork, as I know that the house will have an immediate magic. When first designing a space, I think not only of the floor plan and furniture arrangements but also the look of the walls, imagining pictures climbing to the ceiling. I always tell my clients to just go buy things they like and not worry about where they will go. There will always be a perfect spot.

John and I both love art. Once, when we were at a large antiques fair in Rhinebeck, New York, we went in different directions on the hunt for treasures for our shops. When we met up hours later, John said excitedly that he had bought a picture for us. I also had found a picture I loved. To this day, the early twentieth-century American painting of horses that John discovered hangs on one side of the fireplace, and the small genre painting of a hay wagon that I had unearthed hangs on the other side. They are perfect together. On a trip to India with our friends Jane and Stephen Garmey, each couple started collections of Indian miniature paintings. Theirs hang in their dining room, massed on a wall; ours fill John's dressing room in Punta Cana in the Dominican Republic.

Art collectors of every level are always adding to their collections and rehanging their art as new pieces are acquired. I have never been able to buy very expensive pictures but have bought, little by little, some wonderful things. We mix prints, drawings, oil paintings, watercolors, and photographs. Pieces from the eighteenth century to today are mixed together. The subjects include people, flowers, dogs and other animals, interiors, architecture, landscape, abstracts—whatever we enjoy. What makes things work is how you hang them.

**Not every wall** has to have pictures, but hanging a large picture over a sofa or mantel will give exciting scale to a room.

**Powder rooms and bathrooms** are great places for collections of small pictures.

**If you want to hang pictures** of various sizes together on a wall, measure out the size of the space on the floor and arrange the pictures on the floor so you can see how the group looks together. Then measure and jot down the distance between each picture. This method will make hanging much easier.

**A picture looks best** in a space that fits its size. A tiny picture on a large wall will look lost, just as a large picture in a small space will look out of scale.

# { FIREPLACES }

A FIREPLACE, WHETHER PLACED IN THE MIDDLE or at one end of a room, tends to be a main focus of the space, with furniture grouped around it. So how you treat the mantel or the wall above the fireplace opening becomes very important.

A mirror or painting can be placed over a mantel— the larger the better for dramatic effect. An old fanlight or a piece of modern sculpture also makes a wonderful focal point.

Items on a mantel can be arranged symmetrically or in a more interesting way. This is a place to display special or unusual pieces.

Benches are perfect in front of fireplaces, offering additional seating or a place for books and magazines.

Baskets placed on the side of a fireplace can hold wood and kindling.

During the summer months when fireplaces are not used, they can be emptied and transformed into a display space. Consider arranging large jars of various sizes in the opening or filling it with alabaster containers holding large candles that can be lit for a special effect in the dark fireplace.

I have become a big fan of gas fireplaces. I especially like the logs made by Real-Fyre Gas Logs, which look very realistic, especially when andirons are placed in front of the stack of logs.

# { MIRRORS }

MIRRORS HAVE BEEN USED AS AN IMPORTANT decorative element since the late eighteenth century. Venice has been a center of mirror-making dating back to the thirteenth century, and in the middle of the seventeenth century, the craft spread to England and France, where cabinetmakers created elaborate frames of carved, gilded wood, tortoiseshell, ebony, ivory, or silver.

When used correctly, mirrors can add magic to a space. Here are a few tips:

The larger the mirror, the more dramatic the effect.

Wherever you wish you had a window, hang a mirror. It can provide the same effect.

Because mirrors reflect light, they are a great way to brighten a dark hallway.

To make a narrow room appear wider, place a large mirror on one of the two longer walls.

To make a room seem taller, add a floor-to-ceiling mirror or hang smaller mirrors, one above the other, to the ceiling.

When hanging a mirror over a mantel, tilt it so as to reflect the room, not the ceiling. You may need a block of wood placed between the wall and the mirror and a long hanging wire to achieve the proper angle.

A room can have more than one mirror hanging on different walls.

# { COMFORT }

NOTHING BRINGS ME MORE PLEASURE than seeing John stretched out on the sofa watching a Yankee game or taking a nap with Elizabeth (his beloved whippet) next to him, or having a house guest feel comfortable enough to take a book from the shelf and find a quiet spot somewhere in the house to read. The tiny details are the key to helping anyone find a place to unwind.

Large, upholstered chairs with matching ottomans,
each with a cashmere throw folded over the back and a soft
down pillow, will be irresistible to everyone.

If a room has a bank of large sunny windows, think of building
a window seat and covering it with a seat cushion and lots of soft throw pillows.
What a great place to read, work on a laptop, or just gaze out at the view!

A daybed on a screened porch is a perfect place for an afternoon nap.

A large sofa in front of a sunny window is another little haven of space.

Teak chaises tucked away on a small
out-of-the-way terrace are very inviting.

Always make sure there is proper light for reading.
Standing tensor lights work perfectly.

# CHAPTER III

# Keeping a House Organized

WHEN I WAS A CHILD, MY MOTHER OFTEN would not let me have a friend over to play until I had cleaned up my room, which was always a mess. Trying on all of the clothes in the dress-up trunk or pulling out boxes of beads and making a necklace was much more fun than having to put them all away. I adored the creative part; not so much the tidying-up part. But now I am rather obsessed with organization, mainly because I cannot stand how a messy room looks. Having a place for everything makes it so much easier to put things away. Order is a major part of design, and the more things you have, the more important it is to create places for them.

Wandering through the storage container aisles of stores such as Target, Bed Bath & Beyond, The Container Store, and Kmart is, for me, almost as thrilling as exploring a fabulous antique shop—and much gentler on the pocketbook.

# { LAUNDRY ROOMS }

ANOTHER ROOM IN MY HOUSE that I could not give up is the laundry room. In my home, the laundry room doubles as my project room; it's also used for my flower arranging, gift wrapping, art projects, and extra storage. In many homes, the laundry space is limited to a closet, but if you have a larger room, it can also hold linens and household supplies.

Build cabinets above the washer and dryer for storing cleaning products.

A rod placed over the sink is a perfect place for delicate drip-dry items.

A large worktable or island in the center of a laundry room can be used for ironing large pieces such as sheets or tablecloths. A mattress pad covered with a sheet and upholstered to the top can convert the island to an ironing board.

Two pieces of equipment that are a must for a laundry room are a good clothes steamer and a mangle. The new electric mangles make ironing sheets, tablecloths, napkins, and pillowcases a snap.

Flat baskets are great for sorting clothes and getting the right garments back to the right person.

A movable metal rack in the laundry room is handy for hanging freshly ironed clothes.

# { LINEN CLOSETS }

**O**LDER HOUSES OFTEN HAVE LARGE, WALK-IN LINEN ROOMS with drawers, shelves, and a space for everything. In newer homes, it is rare to find such a specifically designed space, making it even more important to have a linen closet well organized so you can find everything you need and keep necessities on hand.

**Fold a full set of sheets** for each bed together. Place pillowcases inside the folded top and bottom sheets and tie them together with a ribbon. This way each set stays together and the different-size sheets and various styles of pillowcases do not get mixed up. Finding the right set of sheets for each bed will take no time. I also suggest that each set's ribbon correspond to the color of the appropriate bedroom so anyone can find the right sheets for the right bed. Tying the set together also makes it easier to stack on a shelf.

**Sets of towels** should be tied together as well. Over the years, I have found that it is easier to have the same color towel for every bathroom. In our house in the Dominican Republic, I ordered all white towels with a single letter monogram in beige. The towels never get mixed up and they look good in every bathroom. If you have plenty of time or help, towels can be coordinated with the colors of a bathroom.

Place extra blankets and pillows in zippered bags on top shelves to keep them free from dust.

I place other things I need to store in large baskets. I have a basket for light bulbs, one for soaps, and one for extra drugstore items such as Band-Aids, aspirin, toothpaste, and brushes. I hate running out of things.

If you keep table linens in this closet, keep the napkins together in sets with the matching place mats. If you have the space, tablecloths can be folded or hung on hangers, where they will be less creased.

# { CLOTHES CLOSETS }

THERE ARE SO MANY COMMERCIAL COMPANIES that can outfit the interior of a closet and many products that will make it easier to really organize your clothes and maximize the amount of items that a closet can accommodate. Getting the most out of your closets will be worth your time and effort.

Analyze what you need to put in your closet—clothes, shoes, bags, sweaters, etc.—and then plan how to use every inch of space. Make a list and try to figure out how much space you will need for each type of item.

Provide double hanging for jackets, blouses, skirts, and pants folded over. Create a section for long-hanging items, such as coats or pants hung from pants hangers.

Install a section of shelves for folded sweaters, jeans, shirts, exercise clothes, and handbags.

Provide drawers, if there is space, for underclothes, gloves, and scarves. These garments may have to go in a chest of drawers in the bedroom.

In order to use every inch, I put a shelf in the top of my closet with hanging underneath. I have a step stool in every closet so I can reach the top shelves and high-hanging items.

On a shelf where handbags are placed, install a vertical support that creates space for one or two bags. This keeps them from falling over on one another.

Invest in matching hangers. I love the huggable hangers that are narrow and hold any fabric. They are very affordable and will increase the number of pieces that can go on a rod.

For knitted sweaters, I use padded hangers so the shoulders will not stretch. I also like these hangers for jackets and coats.

Under long-hanging pieces, I use clear plastic shoeboxes with pull-out drawers for evening shoes or special shoes I do not wear very often.

Having a place for everything makes putting things away much easier.

Remember: edit, edit, edit. Once a year, take all your clothes out of the closet. Place a hanging rack in your room to hold everything, then make sure you have worn each piece within the year and that it still fits before returning it to the closet.

# { PANTRY }

HAVING A WELL-STOCKED AND ORGANIZED PANTRY will not only make your life easier, but will also allow you to be prepared for unexpected events. You will not need to panic at a sudden call from old friends who happen to be in the neighborhood or your children arriving home at lunchtime with six hungry friends. I cannot tell you the number of times I have invited a group for a meal on the spur of the moment, knowing we could produce something delicious from what we had in the pantry.

Keeping a pantry organized lets you see what you need at a glance so you can quickly make up a shopping list before heading off to Costco or BJ's. Having extras of the things you use the most will keep you from running out of items.

If you are designing a pantry from scratch and have the luxury of a walk-in space, the best design is to have a counter, thirty-six inches high, with shelves below or possibly pull-out bins that make it much easier to use. Refrigerator and freezer drawers are especially useful for holding extra soups and sauces. When we make soup, pasta sauces, or beef stews, we often make double the amount needed and put the extra in the freezer for last-minute meals. If there is space, an under-the-counter wine cooler will ensure that you always have wine on hand.

Put dry ingredients, such as flour, sugars,
rice, and cereals, in tightly sealed plastic containers.

Metal cake tins make great containers for crackers, cookies, and nuts.

Do away with plastic bottles
by installing a filtered-water system and using reusable glass bottles
(we get ours from Crate & Barrel) for your water consumption.

## Items We Always Have

- Cans of whole tomatoes
- Tuna fish in water (especially good Italian brands) and sardines
- Chicken and beef stocks
- Pastas, pastas, and more pastas
- Rice, including white and brown
- Grits

- Cereals
- Duncan Hines double-fudge brownie mix
- Popover mix
- Freezer puff pastry, piecrusts
- Mayonnaise
- Mustards and ketchup
- Tea and coffee
- Cocoa

- Chocolate sauce
- Irish oatmeal
- Virginia peanuts and lots of other kinds of nuts
- Jams and jellies
- Maple syrup
- Chutneys
- Capers
- Tapenade

# { CHINA CLOSETS }

THERE IS SOMETHING VERY SPECIAL TO ME ABOUT CHINA. Whether I am having my coffee and cereal in the morning, fixing tea for a friend, or hosting a dinner party for twelve, I really enjoy choosing the china I want to use. The feel of lovely china and the beauty of a hand-painted leaf on a creamware plate become as much a part of a meal as the food. My passion for china may have started with a miniature tea service I had as a child and used for parties for my dolls. Or maybe it began by helping my mother set the table for dinner.

If you are not sure what china to choose or you just love china, I suggest looking at books on the subject to learn more. The history of china, from the finest hand-painted French plates to hand-thrown pottery from a rural Italian village, is fascinating. England produced many wonderful factories, some still in business, such as Wedgwood and Spode.

Today, young brides will often select a china pattern before really knowing what they will like in the years to come, or how they are going to live. My suggestion is to start with a basic, plain plate or one with a simple colored border. Then you can add salad and dessert plates with different patterns for variety. I love mixing china, but having a basic plate makes this much easier.

If you have collected bits and pieces over the years, I suggest that you put everything you own out on the floor or a big table. What do you use? What do you really like? What did you get for a gift that goes with absolutely nothing? Get rid of what you do not like and do not use. Then see what you may need to add to the pieces you do like to pull them together. A basic white or off-white dinner plate, for instance, can become a background for a blue and white salad plate for a first course. Having china in similar colors makes the mixing much easier and you will have fun setting the table.

Several years ago, on a tour of a shooting plantation in Thomasville, Georgia (now a house museum), I learned that the former owner, Mrs. Parker Poe, had so many china services that guests who came for weeks at a time never saw the same tableware twice, even though they ate three meals a day in the house. I found that amazingly luxurious.

## Stack all matching plates together
and arrange the shelves with similarly colored plates.

## Hang cups from cup hooks
on bottom shelves to maximize storage.

# Basic Necessities (Twelve of Everything)

- Ten-inch dinner plates

- Eight-to-nine-inch salad plates

- Eight-inch dessert plates

- Flat soup plates

- Cups and saucers (I love flat-bottomed cups, as they can be used without saucers as mugs or for tea after dinner.)

- Demitasse cups and saucers

- Small glass bowls for fruit or ice cream

- Bar glasses

- Tall highballs

- Low tumblers

- Champagne flutes

- Table glasses: everyday; flat-bottomed glasses (one large for water, one smaller for wine); small juice glasses; dinner; large-stem glasses for water; medium-size all-purpose stem glasses for wine

- Various-size trays: serving platters (Make sure all your serving platters go together, as they will look better on the buffet.); large, round, fourteen- to sixteen-inch; large rectangular

- Salad bowls—wood and glass

- Teapot, coffeepot, and coffee thermos to keep morning coffee warm

- Various-size pitchers: small ones for milk or cream; medium ones for salad dressings, syrups, and sauces; large ones for juices and ice water

- Sugar bowl and creamer— pottery or china for day; silver for more formal functions

- Small dishes for salt and pepper (I prefer open dishes to the small salt cellars as they are easier to fill. I usually use kosher salt.)

- Various-size bowls for serving salads and fruit

- Gravy boats

- Wine coasters

- Attractive baking dishes that can go directly to the serving table

- Votive candleholders (I can never have too many of these in different colored glass.)

# { USEFUL CONTAINERS }

NOTHING IS MORE HELPFUL FOR KEEPING YOUR HOME ORGANIZED than having special containers for all the things we accumulate during our lives—from pens and sponges, to firewood, cotton balls, umbrellas, magazines, rubber bands, and gardening tools. If all these things are placed neatly in the proper containers, not only can we find them instantly when we need them, but suddenly the mundane will look attractive sitting on a desk or a dresser. A basket organized with current reading material is there for anyone who has a moment to settle into a comfy chair and read a magazine.

I can never have enough containers of various sizes—tall jars and cups, lovely small bowls and dishes, leather folders, baskets, lidded glass jars—to hold the bits and pieces that I want to store. No matter how many of these containers I acquire, they always seem to find a home. My favorite ones at the moment are the exquisite handmade African beaded baskets that we bought in villages while on safari. They now hold paper clips, stamps, and more on my desk.

**Always have a cup** with pencils near every phone for quick messages. Place plain index cards in a small basket for notes.

**To keep a desk tidy,** find leather, fabric, or straw folders to hold bills, letters, or whatever else you may want to save.

**A flat basket** on a table in the library can hold magazines or the day's newspaper.

**Magazine racks** will help keep tabletops free.

**Victorian toast racks** make perfect holders for postcards or note cards. Since we seem to write fewer and fewer letters these days, it is fun to jot a quick note on a postcard. (I still love sending real mail.)

**A large, heavy basket** near the garden can hold clippings and trowels.

**Glass jars with lids** are perfect for cotton balls, Q-tips, or sponges for a dressing table or bathroom vanity.

{ CHAPTER IV }

# Bedrooms
# and Bathrooms

EVERYONE HAS HIS OR HER OWN PERSONAL relationship to the bedroom. For some, it has to be a serene, peaceful space with no television, no books, no distractions. For others, it is a sanctuary, a home within a home. I fall into the latter category. When John is away and I am alone, there is no place I would rather be than in my bedroom—on my bed (with Lucy, my terrier mix). The shelf of my bedside table is filled with books; a basket sits on the floor with all that month's magazines and gardening catalogues; a letter holder has postcards and notepaper for a quick thought to a friend. The phone connects me to my loved ones. There is a thermos of ice water, a photograph of John, an eighteenth-century carved figure of the Virgin Mary that was my mother's, a gardenia-scented candle, a small alarm clock that lights up—helpful when I cannot sleep and wonder what time it is—and, most important, a great lamp with a three-way bulb. The drawer of my bedside table holds everything I may suddenly need, from an emery board to a notepad to aspirin. Across from the bed is a large bookcase with a television, so when I am home, I can watch my favorite shows. Whether it is your room or a guest room, the details are so important to making a bedroom a comfortable and inviting space.

A bedside table must have a great reading light tall enough to be above your book, as well as a bottle of water and a glass, a clock, and tissues in an attractive container.

A writing table can be used by guests as a place to plug in a laptop or as a dressing table.

A bench at the foot of the bed is convenient for holding a suitcase or books and magazines.

A chair or bench next to the bed is a perfect place to drop your robe or put extra reading material.

A flower arrangement or blooming plant will let guests know you have made a special effort for them.

A small flat-screen television will be greatly appreciated by your news-obsessed guests.

Make sure there is a wastebasket in every bedroom.

# { MAKING A PERFECT BED }

ONE OF THE LESSONS ALL THE YOUNG INTERNS IN MY OFFICE learn is how to make a proper bed. If a bed is well made, it stays together better and is easier to remake. Nothing is more luxurious than climbing into a freshly made bed at the end of a busy day. Here are my steps for making the perfect bed:

1. Place a mattress pad on top of the mattress. I love the pillow tops either of down or Dacron, which provide an additional softness to the bed. (I prefer a medium-firm mattress to a very, very hard one.)

2. Put the fitted sheet over the mattress pad.

3. Then put on the top sheet. Start at the bottom, tucking in just enough to go under the mattress; you want more fabric at the top for a longer turnover later.

4. Then comes the blanket. Depending on where you live or the season, a different weight of blanket will be used. In a hot climate, a very lightweight cotton blanket is a good choice. In colder climates, a wool blanket or a lightweight cotton or down comforter will be perfect. I prefer not to use too heavy a blanket, as each person's body temperature is different and the temperature of the room can be adjusted as necessary. Tuck the end of the sheet and blanket using hospital corners. Do not tuck in the top at this point. Cover the blanket or comforter with a blanket cover. I prefer lightly quilted cotton fabrics, such as soft, hand-stitched cotton Indian coverlets that are lightweight and will always look neat. I like the blanket cover to have some body. It makes the top of the bed neater, especially if it has been sat or lain on. Make sure the overhang of the blanket cover is equal on both sides as well as the end. Often, there is excess blanket cover at the top. I fold this over, making a sort of envelope. This is what holds the bedding together.

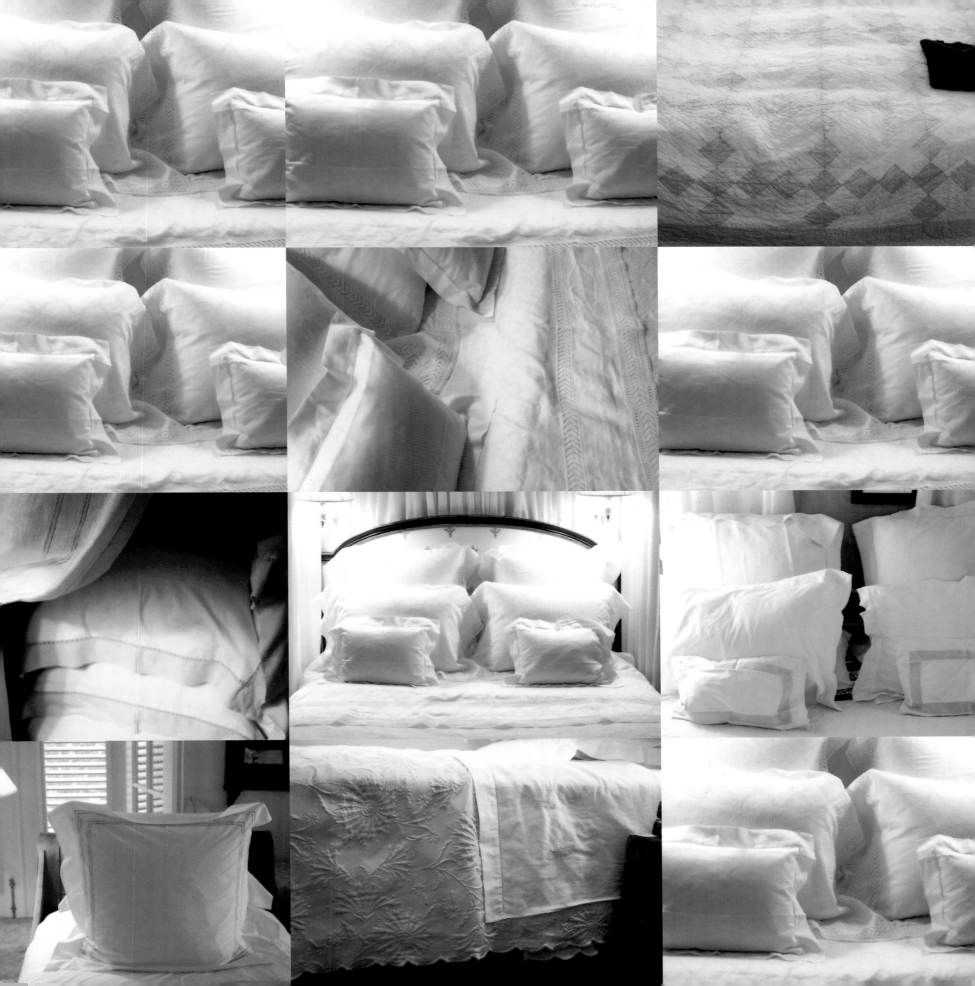

5. Keeping a fourteen-inch space between the top of the sheet and the headboard, turn the top sheet over the blanket. The sheet should come down about one-third of the bed depending on the length of the sheet. I usually leave the top untucked on the sides as it is easier to get into the bed. Make sure the sheets, blanket, and blanket cover are smooth.

6. I use standard-size pillows. On a king-size bed, use six standard, three in a row with three on top. For queen or full, use four standard pillows, one on top of another. I also like to use two square European pillows standing in front of the stack of standard pillows. For the standard pillows, you can use either cases or shams. The European pillows look best with pillow shams. (European pillows give great support if you like to read or watch television in bed.)

7. If you need warmth, place a quilt, cashmere or cotton throw, or down comforter in a duvet cover over the foot of the bed. It is nice to have this extra cover to pull up.

8. For more casual beds, especially for children, a fitted sheet can be used with only a duvet cover over a lightweight down comforter. This is easy and quick to make up.

My favorite sheets are made of four-hundred-to six-hundred-thread-count Egyptian cotton percale. I love their crisp, luxurious texture when you finally get into bed after an exhausting day. I mostly use white sheets, sometimes with embroidered detail coordinating with the color of the bedroom. I am not a fan of dark sheets, but pale colors such as blue, gray, or pink can be very soothing.

# { MAKING A BATHROOM SPECIAL }

AT THE END OF A BUSY DAY, I find nothing more relaxing than soaking in a soothing hot tub with a delicious scent wafting from the water, listening to beautiful music, and letting my mind float.

When I am a guest in someone's house, I am always so appreciative when I see that the hosts have thought of everything for my pleasure and provided special luxuries. When I was planning our house in the Dominican Republic, I made a list of everything we needed in each bath and headed off to Bed Bath & Beyond, Gracious Home, and CVS for a shopping spree.

One of the most important things in a bathroom is storage. When I can design a bathroom from the beginning, I usually include a vanity that has storage below the sink. A medicine cabinet goes above the sink for smaller items. If an existing bath has a pedestal sink, I always try to add a piece of furniture for storage. It is also important in a guest bath to make sure there are places for guests to put their cosmetic bags and shaving kits. A small table can come in handy.

As I love having lots of towels in a bathroom, one towel bar never seems to be adequate. I love the old-fashioned towel racks or stands that you can fill with six or more towels. Small shelves can also hold extra folded towels.

For special touches, collect beautiful small baskets to hold Q-tips or cotton balls. Porcelain bowls or silver cups can do the same. Look for interesting soap dishes—alabaster, porcelain, or even a big shell looks wonderful filled with soaps. A tissue box should always be covered, or take the tissues out of the box and put them in a flat basket.

# Stock guest bathrooms with travel-size products that guests may have forgotten. Buy small guest soaps and throw them out after each set of visitors so there is always fresh soap. Old soap is not very appealing to a new guest.

## Necessities

- Vanity or cabinet
- Hair dryer
- Shower cap
- Extra towels
- Toilet paper
- Tampons
- Aspirin
- Band-Aids
- Nail file
- Shaving cream
- Razors
- Toothpaste
- Toothbrushes

- Body lotions
- Small deodorant
- Suntan lotion / sunblock
- Hair spray
- Scent diffuser
- Terry-cloth robe
- Hooks on door
- Water glasses
- Basket or small tiered table next to toilet with extra toilet paper, magazines, tampons, moist wipes
- Wastebaskets

- Laundry hamper or laundry bag on back of door
- Scale
- Magnifying mirror, either on a stand or attached to a wall

### TUB/SHOWER

- Special scented soaps or natural mild soaps
- Body washes
- Sponge/loofah
- Bath oils
- Shampoo
- Conditioner

{ CHAPTER V }

# Personal Touches

WHETHER FAMILY PHOTOGRAPHS, a collection of unique pottery, an amazing painting hanging over the sofa, or a dog bed tucked under a table, there is nothing that brings a home to life more than unique personal touches—especially if they are displayed in an organized and interesting manner. A special ivory box from a trip to India, a bronze sculpture of a dog, a small silver wheelbarrow, or a hand-blown piece of pottery will tell you something about the occupant.

Of course, everyone has a different sensibility as to how they want their home to feel. Some people are minimalist and choose to be very, very disciplined about editing their possessions. Tables will be empty, books put away on shelves. If young children live in a home, there probably will not be lots of small, fragile objects waiting for disaster to happen.

The person who cannot resist stopping at an antique shop on the way to a friend's house for lunch will probably have some kind of collection displayed somewhere in his or her home. Whatever way we choose to live, our homes show so much about us. For that reason, we should give a lot of thought to the smallest details of our rooms.

# { PHOTOGRAPHS }

THANKS TO DIGITAL CAMERAS and the ease of home printing, people are taking more pictures than ever before. Some people have the time and discipline to put these pictures into beautifully organized albums or labeled boxes. But the tendency is to put them in inexpensive frames all over the house. This drives me crazy, as it clutters every surface.

I love having pictures in my home, but it is important
to first edit them. I often see that people have put out too many similar pictures. You do
not need to display every photo you took on a trip or at an event. I like to group pictures
together on one or two surfaces in a room—not every space. The frames
look better if they are similar and all silver, all wood, or a mixture of two types—
maybe silver frames with leather frames. If there are too many types of frames,
it is hard to make them look attractive together. In a modern room, clear Lucite frames
of different sizes look great together.

Place personal pictures, such as the children as babies or dear family
members, where you will really see them and remember the events;
the photographs should mean something to you. I like to choose a very special
picture and print it in a large size—say eight by ten inches
or five by seven inches—to mix with several smaller pictures.

If you have many, many photos, think of framing them all the same way and
hanging them in a hall or up a staircase. Group several together to make one larger picture
or have a small picture blown up to eight by ten inches or nine by twelve inches.

# { LIVING WITH ANIMALS }

OKAY, BY NOW, IF YOU HAVE READ ANY OF MY BOOKS, you must know I love my dogs. But I am also aware that not everyone who comes to our house shares the passion we have for our pets. How we live with our animals must be considered so as to make sure our homes are pleasant for everyone. It is essential when you come into a home that you are not greeted by the smell of kitty litter or damp musty dogs. Cats clean themselves, but dogs need maintenance. Brushing a furry coat and giving regular baths are essential.

Even though our dogs have the run of the house, they also have their favorite spots, especially when we are away. In our New York apartment, we have dog beds under the front hall table where I always find Lucy and Elizabeth when we come home. A large Chinese fishbowl is filled with fresh water nearby, so they are completely content. Our dear friends Jonathan and Stiles, who have a large group of dogs, built wonderful pens with gates under a long counter in their mudroom. Each dog has his or her own little room with a soft bed, and they run right in when their owners are leaving for a few hours. This keeps them out of mischief and protects the house.

One of the most creative solutions to where to put the kitty litter was created by my friend Stephen Garmey, who cut out the silhouette of a cat at the bottom of the door to the closet where the cat box is kept. The litter is out of sight, and Henry the cat knows exactly where to go.

Empty and store large bags of dog food in containers, such as galvanized cans with tight lids or large covered plastic bins. If you have different food for different dogs, store the food in separate smaller containers with each dog's name on it.

Have a large basket nearby to hold the dog toys.

If you let animals on sofas and chairs, as we do, protect your furniture. Find fake-fur throws to cover the seat and back of a sofa or a cotton quilt that blends with the colors of your room. These can easily be put in the washer and kept fresh. Make the protection look like a part of the decoration. No one wants to sit on a sofa or chair with old sheets thrown over it.

Provide dog beds in the rooms you spend time in. Your animals want to be with you, and if you provide them with their own comfortable spot, they are less likely to want yours.

Always provide a bed for your dog near the door from which you come and go.

**Find interesting flat-bottomed** heavy bowls for water. I put them in the kitchen and any room in which the dogs sleep. Small Chinese fishbowls or the bottom of a porcelain tureen work perfectly.

**Have a hook for leashes** near the door or a basket to roll them up in.

**Sisal carpet is not good for dog owners,** as the broken fiber is very absorbent and will hold a stain. Sea grass, a natural, whole fiber, is much more forgiving.

**Save some extra fabric** from a piece of furniture in your room and have a cover made for a dog bed. Fake-fur dog beds look great in any room. Think of the bed as a piece of furniture for your four-legged friends.

**Keep towels near the door** to dry off wet dogs and clean their feet if they are wet or dirty.

# { COLLECTIONS }

A PASSION FOR COLLECTING OFTEN STARTS EARLY IN LIFE, perhaps with dolls, action figures, or baseball cards, and can become a very addictive hobby. Or it may come later in life, as we develop a love of objects such as porcelains, silver, and art. Collecting may be an extension of other hobbies—sports, gardening, sailing, a love of animals, or reading. The shells we find on our walks on the beach or the delicate bird's nest we discover nestled in a shrub while working in the garden can begin a collection of natural treasures.

In our travels we often find beautiful handmade pieces. Every day when I look at the delicate beaded baskets that hold cotton balls and safety pins on my dressing table I think of the women who wove them. I will never forget buying these baskets, which were laid out on cotton cloths in vibrant prints in front of handmade mud and straw homes belonging to these elegant women. A carved wooden rooster found on a roadside in Jamaica mixes with a brightly painted pottery charger we puchased in the Souk in Marrakesh.

Once we get started, we get caught up in the hunt. We read and study; we go to museums; we search at shows, shops, and auctions. The search becomes so enjoyable that it is often hard to stop. And, of course, if you have a name like Bunny—well, you can imagine.

**Build shelves,** or look for interesting cabinets or freestanding bookcases to hold collections.

**If you collect more than one type of object—** china, pieces of silver, a collection of bronzes—group like things together. It will make more of an impact.

**Unrelated items can be grouped** together by color: all green, all white, all orange. Even if things are made of different materials and subjects, the color will unite the otherwise mismatched group.

**I often try to arrange** a group of unrelated things in interesting ways. Sometimes "opposites," such as a lovely piece of porcelain next to a very primitive carved figure, or a soft-worn pewter plate combined with a Chinese porcelain figure, can make an eye-pleasing display. Explore mixing different shapes and finishes.

**Groupings should be arranged** with a careful sense of design. Large pieces should be set in the back. Pairs of things can be put together balanced by a single large piece. It is fun to arrange and rearrange to make a captivating display.

**It is important to remember** that a tabletop has to have at least enough empty space to hold a glass or cup. Do not fill every surface. Try to display objects on shelves or in glass cabinets as well.

{ CHAPTER VI }

# Maintenance

# { HOUSEKEEPING }

**T**AKING CARE OF YOUR HOME is as important as decorating it. Nothing is sadder than going into a house that is dirty, dusty, or generally unkempt. Maintenance is a must; by properly taking care of your house and its contents, everything will last much longer.

Here are some housekeeping tips I have learned over the years that help with recurring problems:

## Dusting: Use soft yellow dustcloths with a bit of lemon oil;
the new microfiber cloths also work well. Never use products such as Pledge, as they can leave a buildup of film over time that may discolor wood.

## Polishing silver: Clean items with silver polish like Goddard's.
Dry each piece thoroughly and store in a plastic storage bag, squeezing all the air out before closing. This will keep the silver sparkling.

# Red wine stains

Always have Wine Away, ammonia, talcum powder, or salt, and a spray bottle on hand. If you don't have a product like Wine Away, staple pantry items can be used to lift wine spills.

- To remove a stain from a cotton or linen tablecloth, blot the stain and cover it with salt or talcum powder so you can deal with the stain after guests have left.

- To remove a stain from carpet, blot the stain, then spray it with a solution of one part ammonia to two parts warm water. Let sit for five to ten minutes. Blot and repeat if necessary.

# Wax removal

Since I have spent hours of my life removing wax from tablecloths and tabletops, I no longer use unprotected candlesticks. All my candles are now in hurricane holders or have hurricane shades. I also use only votive candles on the table. However, in case wax does spill, there are ways to remove it from fabric and wood.

- To remove wax from fabric: Let wax dry. Apply an ice pack (or cubes of ice wrapped in a towel) for several minutes until wax is very cold and hard. Using a credit card or thin butter knife, scrape off what you can. For the remaining wax, cover both sides of the fabric with a paper bag. Gently iron the area until the wax is absorbed into the paper. You may have to repeat this step.

- To remove wax from furniture: Use the same ice technique and carefully scrape off the wax. Remove the remainder of the wax by rubbing cream furniture wax over the spot with a clean cloth.

- To prevent wax from sticking to glass: Pour just enough water to cover the bottom of votives and hurricanes to prevent the wax from sticking. I also often use tea lights that have a foil base. If wax does melt on the glass, place the candleholder in the freezer; after several hours, the wax should be frozen and easily scraped off with a dull knife.

# To remove water rings and heat marks

White rings on wood furniture may look disastrous, but they can usually be erased with a few simple steps.

- Mix one tablespoon baking soda or ashes into a small amount of mayonnaise and cover the white stain. Rub in and leave on for several hours. Rub off with paper towels.

- Put wax paper over the water mark and heat your iron to the lowest setting. Place a T-shirt or towel over the wax paper and gently iron the spot until it disappears.

# Living with animals

All I can say is, buy gallons of Nature's Miracle, just in case.

# Books

It is important to periodically remove all books from shelves and carefully dust them. Leatherbound books should have leather conditioning rubbed into the covers to keep them from drying out.

# Heat and humidity

Temperature and humidity levels in a home probably have the most detrimental effects on furniture, books, and even art. In our house in Connecticut, I am always running humidifiers to help counteract the dryness of the central heat. In the Dominican Republic, we have the opposite problem: too much moisture. It is so important to keep humidity levels balanced in the winter so that everything does not dry up, including people. Overheating a house is not good for the house, the furniture, the people, or the environment. In a damp climate, run dehumidifiers and use fans to circulate the air. Mildew is as harmful to a home as too much heat.

- Use humidifiers or dehumidifiers as necessary, depending on the season and where you live, to counter the impact of too much or too little moisture on furniture, books, and art.

{ CHAPTER VII }

# Entertaining

Ⓜ️Y LOVE OF ENTERTAINING CAME, I am sure, from the wonderful memories I have from my childhood, both of helping my mother plan my birthday parties and the excitement of going to friends' parties. The large Sunday lunches given by my great-aunt Berta Jones, where all generations of the family got together, were something I looked forward to every week. I was lucky to grow up in a place where entertaining at home was the norm. There were not a lot of restaurants in Charlottesville, Virginia, where I grew up, and as Albemarle County was dry and you could not get a drink in a public place, everyone entertained privately. Things are different now and we are all busy, yet there is nothing more rewarding than having friends and family together in your home.

Nothing shows a person's kindness more than entertaining. Entertaining is a gift a host gives friends and family. On a book tour in California, my dear friend Suzanne Rheinstein gave me a large buffet dinner in her beautiful home in Los Angeles to introduce me to her friends and other people in the design community. Suzanne is a masterful hostess. She makes entertaining seem effortless, and because she is organized, thoughtful, and creative, her parties are magical.

When I was back in Charlottesville for a speaking engagement, my cousin Missy Sanford gave a cocktail party in my honor. Friends and family I had not seen in years, including an old boarding school chum and a dear friend of my parents, were there. Afterward, a smaller group was invited for a delicious buffet dinner. The night was particularly special because I had practically grown up in this house, which belonged to Missy's mother, Porte, who was my godmother.

At Christmas, over one hundred people wait for their invitations to my friends Lee and Fritz Link's party in their New York apartment. Everyone looks forward to seeing one another; some friends you only see there, once a year, dipping into Lee's delicious eggnog. No one leaves hungry, as the dining table is heaped with tempting food. And in case you don't get to the buffet, trays of shrimp, tea sandwiches, and cheese puffs are passed around.

The warm memories I have are because Missy and Jack, Suzanne and Fred, and Lee and Fritz made the effort to give the gift of these cozy parties. These are all people who entertain beautifully; they plan, prepare, and anticipate what is needed for making a special evening for their guests. They also entertain often, and in this case practice does make perfect.

# { PLANNING PARTIES }

I COULD NOT WAIT TO START ENTERTAINING when I had my first apartment in New York, which I shared with an old friend from home. In a small space, we would make a casserole and salad and invite other single friends who would bring a bottle of wine and, we hoped, another single friend. It was a fabulous way to meet new people. After I was married and living in a small apartment, I would serve buffets from the kitchen where everyone would help themselves to a plate and sit around the living room, as we had no dining table. Later, when I had a larger house, I could have more formal dinners. But what was always important was to plan a party that worked for the space and budget at hand so it was fun for everyone. A host should never seem stressed and should be able to enjoy the party along with everyone invited.

Where do the coats go? What will your guests eat? How will you serve the food? What will there be to drink? Think out the whole event, from the time people arrive until they leave, and then begin to prepare and plan.

1. Only host a party that you can easily handle. Do not make it more complicated than it needs to be. Keeping things simple will allow you to have a better time.

2. A cocktail party with a buffet allows for a more casual party and can be done with less help. Serve food that is easy to eat.

3. Make lists, lists, and more lists to ensure that you have everything ready beforehand and that you have what you need, from a coatrack to cocktail napkins.

4. If you are serving a meal, make sure there are enough places for everyone to sit to eat their food. No one should have to stand or sit on the floor.

5. Afternoon tea parties are great for families. Kids can have hot chocolate with tiny peanut butter and honey sandwiches, the husbands can watch football, and the girls—well, they always like to get together.

6. Picnics are another great way to entertain families. Pack up sandwiches, fried chicken, potato chips, and brownies and go to the backyard or the park for a great summer afternoon.

7. If you are able to hire a caterer or help for a large party, meet them and have them cater a small party first so they can get to know you, your house, and how you like things done. You want to be sure the party represents you, not how someone else thinks you should entertain.

# { COCKTAIL PARTIES }

Make sure the food is passed in small, bite-size pieces.
It is almost impossible to eat off a plate and hold a glass or be served at the same time.

If there is no bartender, set up small bars in different rooms
so your guests can help themselves.

Place food around the house as well as on the dining table
so guests can pick up something wherever they are. Bowls of nuts and olives, platters of
crudités, and cheese straws can be on small tables.

# { SEATED DINNERS }

A T OUR HOUSE IN CONNECTICUT, John and I always have seated dinners. We serve the food on a long buffet where the guests help themselves and then go to the table where there is a place card for each guest. I spend a lot of time thinking about the seating, which shows consideration for your guests. I always separate couples and try to place people next to each other who I think will have something in common. If one of my guests is a quiet person, I try to put him or her next to someone who is very outgoing.

The wine is placed in wine coasters for guests to help themselves, and water glasses are refilled throughout the meal. We have someone pass the food for seconds, then clear the table and serve dessert so that no one has to get up. After dessert, we move to the living room for coffee and tea, and maybe some chocolates.

For a formal dinner served at the table, it is very important to have help that is professional and knows how to serve properly. There are several real pros we call upon for help who know us, our house, and how we like things done.

# { BUFFETS }

For a buffet where people may be eating off their laps, serve food that does not need cutting, such as a bourguignonne or meatloaf—food that can be eaten with a fork.

Wrap a knife and fork in a linen napkin, tie with a pretty ribbon, and put them in a basket so your guests can easily carry them when finding their place to eat.

Have someone checking the plates and taking them to the kitchen when they are empty. This is something you can often lure your teenagers to help with.

Make sure to refill wine or water glasses regularly.

Put out dessert and have guests help themselves.

Only have two courses with a buffet. John and I use large dinner plates and usually offer our guests three or four choices of dishes (a meat, two vegetables, and a starch). The table is then cleared and a dessert is served on small plates.

# { NECESSITIES TO HAVE ON HAND }

THE MORE PREPARED YOU ARE, the easier it will be to entertain—even at the last minute. Knowing you have what you need on hand will give you the confidence to say "Come for dinner tomorrow."

Plan which glasses you will use, the way you will set the table, how you will serve dinner and on what, and everything will fall into place for a fabulous, relaxing occasion for you and your guests. Put items out ahead of time; see how everything looks and what more you need for the number of people you are having.

## Plates

- Ten-and-a-half-inch dinner plates

- Eight-to-nine-inch dessert and salad plates. (I prefer a nine-inch plate, which is harder to find, because it is more generous for a salad or first-course plate.)

- Eleven-inch chargers or service plates for formal entertaining. (We sometimes use the larger plates if we are having a buffet, as John usually makes a number of different dishes.)

- Always purchase one or two extra plates in case there is an accident. I suggest having twelve of each set.

- Do not be afraid to use different styles of plates on the buffet for large groups. Matching plates should be used for a seated dinner, although a different pattern can be used for each course.

- Coffee cups and saucers

- Demitasse cups and saucers

## Glasses

- Basic "all-purpose" wine glasses

- Water glasses

- White wine glasses

- Champagne glasses

- Brandy snifters

- Highballs or tall glasses (I use these for iced tea and lemonade.)

- Low tumblers (I prefer these for cocktails.)

## Serving platters

- At least four round or oval platters that will work together on a buffet table; they should all be the same color

- At least four good serving dishes that can go from oven to table; they should work with the serving platters

- Salad bowls—wood, glass, or china

# Flatware

- Dinner knives and forks

- Salad/dessert forks—double the quantity, as you may need one fork for salad or a first course and one for dessert after a meal

- Small knives for first course or cheese course

- Tablespoons—double the quantity, as you may need one for soup and one for dessert after a meal

- Teaspoons for coffee/tea

- Demitasse spoons for afternoon coffee (I always offer decaf coffee and herbal tea as well.)

- Salt and pepper holders: I prefer tiny open bowls with loose, coarse salt and pepper. They are easier to fill and use. I have them in glass, porcelain, and lacquer. (Note that salt will corrode silver, so the holders must be emptied and cleaned after each meal.)

- Wine coasters, at least two per person

- Pitchers—glass, silver, or pottery for water, iced tea, or lemonade

- Votive candleholders (I have many sets of these, as I love the light they give to the dinner table. Clear glass works with everything, although I have them in amber glass, mercury glass, porcelain, silver, and red glass for Christmas.)

# Table linens

- Nothing can change the look of your table more than a new tablecloth, napkins, or place mats. By having table linens in a variety of contrasting colors, complementary patterns, and interesting textures, you can transform your table setting from everyday to party-ready.

- Consider using Burberry-patterned napkins with straw place mats for a country lunch. Simple cotton place mats can make a setting more casual, whereas beautiful Belgian linen mats are more elegant. We often place our blue and white china on a hot pink linen tablecloth, and our brown pottery looks fabulous on apple green

- Place mats—straw, linen, cotton, lacquer, leather, or cork

- Tablecloths—solid colors from white to any colors you like that work with your china

- Indian bedspreads make wonderful, inexpensive tablecloths. Buy a twin size if you have a narrow table, and buy two if one is not long enough and simply overlap in the middle.

- It is hard to find large, square cloths for round tables. A king-size bedspread makes a perfect tablecloth for a sixty- to sixty-six-inch round table. I like square cloths on round tables as I think it looks like a tablecloth, not a skirted table.

- You can never have too many plain white napkins. I especially love extra-large damask napkins, which are wonderful for a buffet when people are eating off their laps. I often find lovely cloth napkins in antique malls or thrift shops.

# { SETTING THE TABLE }

**Y**EARS AGO, I TORE OUT A PICTURE from *Vogue* of a table setting done by the very stylish Pauline de Rothschild. In the center of a very, very long table covered in faded Indian bed covers there was a grand wooden carousel horse under which she had placed masses of topiaries in small blue and white Chinese jars. I have been inspired by that magical table and enthralled with creating interesting table settings ever since.

I look at each table as an empty canvas on which I can build a new still life. By combining your china with different table linens, objects, and flowers, you can always create a bit of magic. I love to place items from around the house with small flower arrangements or intersperse potted succulents with votives down the length of the table. Pieces from my rabbit collection and vases of spring bouquets make a lovely Easter centerpiece. In the fall, I might scatter pumpkins and gourds down the center of the table.

Make sure to keep flowers or decorative objects low so that guests can easily see over them. Conversely, if you have a tall centerpiece, guests should be able to see under it. Always sit in every seat to make sure there is nothing in the way of guests being able to easily talk to or see one another.

Having the correct props makes building centerpieces so much more fun and allows you to create a variety of table settings appropriate for any occasion. Add to your linen collection so that you have both solid colors and small patterns. I love to mix colors, such as yellow tulips on an apple-green linen cloth with green and white plates. Or I will choose a deep pink tablecloth to go with blue and white plates, or maybe a cloth made from simple burlap with all white plates and white hydrangeas in simple basket containers.

Once you have decorated your table, set out the dishes as well as the proper knives and forks for the meal you plan to serve.

A large dinner knife should always be placed on the right side of the plate and a large dinner fork on the left side of the plate.

If you have a first course, such as salad or smoked salmon, you need to include a small fork and knife.

If the first course is soup, place a large soup spoon on the right side next to the dinner knife.

A dessert fork and spoon should be placed at the top of the plate.

Place the napkin between the knife and fork.

Each place should have a large glass for water and a smaller glass for wine. If you serve different wines for each course, you may need two wine glasses. (I usually use only one wine glass but serve both red and white wine and let guests help themselves.)

For a buffet, dinner plates can be set on the serving table for each guest to fill and bring to the dining table. For more formal dinners, you can set a large service plate on top of which first-course and dinner plates are placed.

It is very nice to have small salt-and-pepper sets for each guest placed above the dessert fork and spoon, or at least a set between every two guests.

# { BAR }

IN WHATEVER ROOM YOU USE THE MOST—your living room, family room, or library—I suggest having a bar that can freely be used. If you want a drink, it is nice to have a bar nearby, and having refills at hand is so much easier than running to the kitchen each time a glass is empty.

Growing up in the South where entertaining was constant—people even dropped by unannounced—I learned to be ready. My great-aunt Berta had the most wonderful American pine corner cupboard in her living room. During the day, the doors were closed, but about five o'clock in the evening, the doors would be opened. Inside were shelves with glasses of various sizes and a complete supply of sodas, fruit juices, and an assortment of liquors; a silver ice bucket and a pitcher of water were brought in, and she was ready to receive guests. We all felt comfortable helping ourselves.

Mahogany three-tiered trolleys make great bars. The top can hold a tray with glasses and an ice bucket, and lower shelves can hold cans of sodas, juices, and bottles of water. Narrow cabinets are also perfect for a drinks area with storage in the bottom cupboards.

# { MENUS }

SINCE WE DO LIKE TO ENTERTAIN, both John and I love reading recipes and cookbooks. We are always tearing recipes out of a paper or magazine that sound interesting. If I have something delicious to eat in a friend's house, I will ask for the recipe, but from then on I always refer to the dish as "Jane's potpie" or "Inge's soufflé." If we go to a restaurant and order a particularly good dish, we try to figure out what is in it and then try it at home. As we often entertain casually, we try to have main dishes that can be made ahead of time. Then just before we serve dinner, we can cook the pasta, rice, or orzo and immediately serve it piping hot on a large, round, colorfully striped Moroccan platter with sprinkled parsley as a garnish.

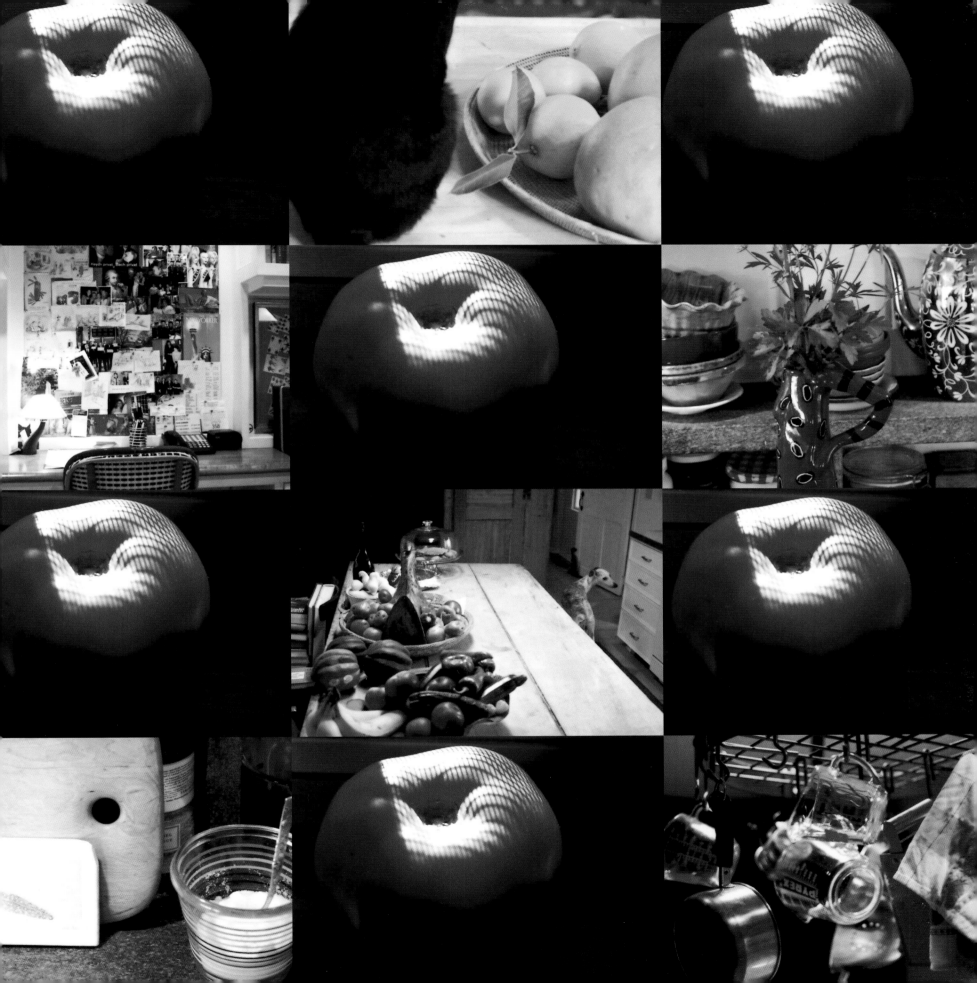

# Cocktail Buffet

Small biscuits with thin-sliced
country ham

Fresh shrimp with cocktail sauce

Crudités with herb dip or hummus

Tiny sandwiches made with thin-sliced
white bread (cut the crust off),
cucumber, pimento cheese, tomatoes,
or tuna fish salad

Platters of thin-sliced Italian meats and
cheeses such as pepperoni, salami, salsiccia,
prosciutto, pancetta, coppa, Pecorino
Romano, Parmesan, cheddar, Gouda cut
into cubes, or a soft triple-crème cheese

Large, flat baskets of sliced French
and Italian breads

Bowls of mixed olives

Country paté with bread

# Summer Lunch

Tomato aspic with shrimp or chicken salad

Cold rice salad

Peach cobbler with whipped cream

# Fall or Winter Lunch

Casserole fish chowder

Green salad with pear, soft cheese
(Brie, St. André), and French bread

Fresh fruit with cookies
(Tate's cookies are especially delicious)
or coconut cake

# Dinner I

Lamb or Beef Tajine

Orzo with peas

Chopped green salad

Vanilla ice cream with Grand Marnier and
chopped nuts (almonds or pistachios)

Brownies

# Dinner II

Rotisserie chicken served with
hot pepper jelly on the side

Scalloped potatoes

Roasted vegetables
(Brussels sprouts, broccoli, small white
onions, yellow peppers)

Apple pie with crème fraîche

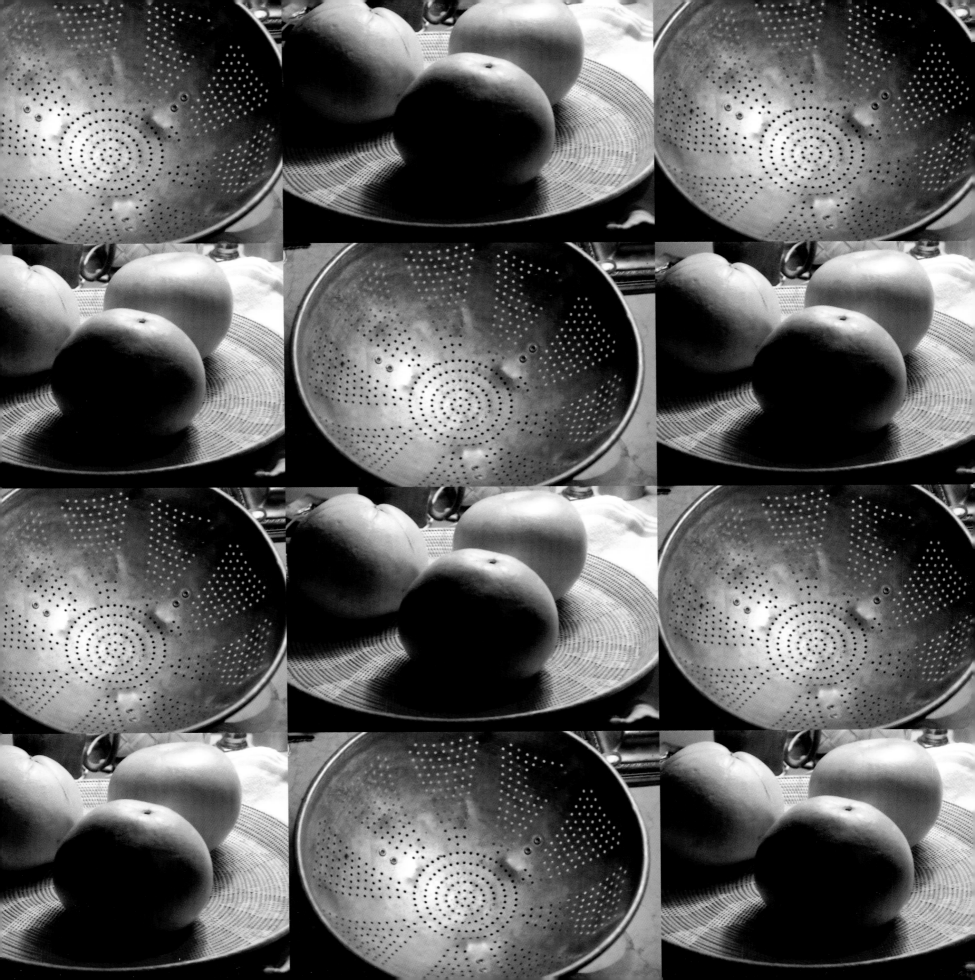

# { RECIPES }

## Tomato Aspic

*I love the texture of this spicy tomato aspic, which we serve in the summer with either chicken or shrimp salad. Make the aspic the day before in a round ring mold.*

2 envelopes of unflavored gelatin
1 large onion, chopped
3 stalks of celery, chopped
4 cups of V8 juice
freshly ground pepper
¼ teaspoon salt
2 teaspoons tarragon vinegar

1. Soak the gelatin in ½ cup cold water.

2. Put the onion, celery, V8 juice, pepper, and salt in a saucepan to boil and simmer slowly for 10 minutes. Add the gelatin and vinegar.

3. Wipe out a ring mold with salad oil and pour the mixture into mold. Put in the refrigerator overnight.

4. The next day, place the mold quickly in warm water, place a large round dish over mold, and turn upside down. Put shrimp or chicken salad in the center and decorate around the sides with lettuce or spinach leaves.

## Casserole Fish Chowder

*This chowder is very, very easy, and makes a delicious lunch.*

2 pounds, fresh fish, boned, skinned, and cut in chunks (use haddock, whitefish, halibut, or cod)
4 potatoes, thinly sliced
3 onions, thinly sliced
A few celery leaves, finely chopped
1 bay leaf
1 garlic clove, minced
4 whole cloves
¼ teaspoon dill seed
2½ teaspoons salt
¼ teaspoon white pepper
¼ cup butter
½ cup dry white wine
2 cups heavy cream

1. Combine all the ingredients, except for the cream, with two cups of water in a 3-quart casserole.

2. Cover the casserole and bake for 1 hour at 350°F.

3. Heat the cream to scalding and stir into the chowder. Garnish with fresh parsley or dill and serve.

Makes ten cups or eight servings

# Jane Garmey's Supremely Simple Red Cabbage and Kielbasa

1 large red cabbage (4 to 5 pounds)
2 tablespoons olive oil
3 large onions, coarsely chopped
5 cloves garlic, coarsely chopped
3 large green apples, peeled and cored,
   chopped into ½-inch cubes
1 cup brown sugar
1 cup wine vinegar
Two 14-ounce packages of kielbasa
sausage, sliced into rounds ½ inch thick
1 cup pitted prunes
12 whole cloves
½ teaspoon anise
salt and pepper
sour cream
1 bunch dill, finely chopped

1. Chop the cabbage into coarse strips, discarding the center knob. In a large cast-iron casserole dish sauté the cabbage in the oil for 3 to 5 minutes. Add the onions, garlic, and apples.

2. Dissolve the brown sugar in the vinegar and pour into the casserole dish. Add the kielbasa, prunes, cloves, anise, and a little salt and ground pepper.

3. Cover and cook for about 1½ hours in a 300°F oven. Check occasionally, and add vinegar if the cabbage looks too dry.

4. Remove the casserole from the oven and ladle the cabbage and kielbasa into bowls. Top with a heaping spoonful of sour cream and chopped dill (lots of it!) and serve with black bread on the side.

Makes six to eight servings

## { CHAPTER VIII }

# Making Your Own Scrapbook

OVER THE YEARS, I HAVE COLLECTED IDEAS on decorating, entertaining, and gardening, as well as tips on repairing objects, selecting furniture, and organization. I tear pages from a magazine or scan from a book and group them together by subject. Though I admire people who can create really beautifully arranged scrapbooks, my inspirations are kept in red binders in simple heavyweight sheet protectors that I purchase at Staples. Each subject has its own binder or, in some cases, several binders, and I periodically go through and edit images in order to keep the collection fresh.

I also include eight-by-ten-inch copies of inspiring trip photographs in the binders so I can refer to them again. For instance, I have a scrapbook dedicated to photos of paintings with especially inspiring color combinations from museums around the world. These scrapbooks have done so much to train my eye and influence my own creativity.

However you want to make your own scrapbooks, it is important to just begin. You never know when you will want inspiration for your own home or garden. The images that have caught your attention will always be there for you to refer to.

# { INSPIRATIONS }

I CARRY A SMALL CAMERA IN MY BAG WITH ME WHEREVER I GO. I never leave home without it, because I never know when I might see an unusual stone floor pattern or a beautiful rare plant, or be inspired by a piece of furniture. I may photograph a pattern or a piece of embroidery that I could translate into a rug design. I am always looking for new ideas. When I get home, I print out the pictures and sort them into different categories—gardening, decorating, color combinations, architecture, furniture, patterns. They either go into boxes with subject labels or into my red notebooks. It is very convenient to have your boxes or notebooks near a large table where you can spread the images out and remember the wonderful things you have seen. Taking pictures of things you love is the best way to educate your eye.

Inspiration can come from so many places. Attend a lecture given by someone you admire. Go on local house or garden tours. Watch Ina Garten on the Food Network. Subscribe to magazines; I cannot wait for mine to arrive each month. Buy as many books as you can—a library is always a great source of inspiration. And travel, travel, travel; the world offers so many treasures.

# { FAVORITE BOOKS }

## Decoration

*Jacques Grange: Interiors*
by Pierre Passebon

*Vogue Living: Houses, Gardens, People*
by Hamish Bowles

*Rooms* by Derry Moore

*Albert Hadley: The Story of America's
Preeminent Interior Designer*
by Adam Lewis

*Defining Luxury: The Qualities of Life at Home*
by Jeffrey Bilhuber

*Decorating with Antiques: Confidently
Combining Old and New*
by Caroline Clifton-Mogg and
Fritz von der Schulenberg

*The Southern Cosmopolitan: Sophisticated
Southern Style*
by Susan Sully

*Timeless Interiors*
by Axel Vervoordt

*Style and Substance: The Best of Elle Décor*
by Margaret Russell

## Housekeeping

*Martha Stewart's Homekeeping Handbook:
The Essential Guide to Caring for Everything
in Your Home*
by Martha Stewart

*Home Comforts: The Art and Science
of Keeping House*
by Cheryl Mendelson

## Cookbooks

*Joy of Cooking*
by Irma S. Rombauer

*The Barefoot Contessa Cookbook*
by Ina Garten

*Essentials of Classic Italian Cooking*
by Marcella Hazan

*Chez Panisse Menu Cookbook*
by Alice Waters

*The Gift of Southern Cooking: Recipes and
Revelations from Two Great American Cooks*
by Edna Lewis and Scott Peacock

*How to Cook Everything:
2,000 Simple Recipes for Great Food*
by Mark Bittman

*The King Arthur Flour Baker's Companion:
The All-Purpose Baking Cookbook*
by King Arthur Flour

# { RESOURCES }

## FURNITURE

**Kenny Ball Antiques,** www.kennyballantiques.com

**Ballard Designs**, www.ballarddesigns.com

**Lars Bolander,** www.larsbolander.com

**Circa Interior and Antiques,** www.circaonline.net

**Charles Faudree,** www.charlesfaudree.com

**1stbids,** www.1stdibs.com

**Halcyon House Antiques,** Baltimore, MD

**Hollyhock,** www.hollyhockinc.com

**Mrs. Howard,** www.phoebehoward.net

**Mary Evelyn McKee Interiors,** www.maryevelyn.com

**Mecox Gardens,** www.mecoxgardens.com

**Paysage,** www.paysage.com

**Restoration Hardware,**
www.restorationhardware.com

**John Rosselli Antiques and Decoration,**
www.johnrosselliantiques.com

**Mark Simmons Interiors,**
www.marksimmonsinteriors.com

**Summerfields Interior Design,** www.
summerfieldsnaples.com

## FABRICS

**John Robshaw,** www.johnrobshaw.com

**John Rosselli,** www.johnrosselliassociates.com

**Tea Tree Fabrics,** www.aletaonline.com

## CHINA

**Crate and Barrel,** www.crateandbarrel.com

**Treillage,** www.treillageny.com

## FIREPLACE ACCESSORIES

**Jefferson Brass,** www.jeffersonbrass.com

## DOG SUPPLIES

**Harry Barker,** www.harrybarker.com

**Wally Beds,** www.wallybed.com

## BOOKS

**Alibris,** www.alibris.com

**Archivia Books,** www.archiviabooks.com

**Hayden & Fandetta Rare Books,**
www.haydenandfandettararebooks.com/

**Johnny Cake Books,** www.johnnycakebooks.com

**Potterton Books,** www.pottertonbooksusa.com

**Strand,** www.strandbooks.com

## FOOD

**Caroline Cakes,** www.carolinecakes.com

**Crab Cakes,** www.crabcakes.com

**Italian meats,** www.ditalia.com

# { PHOTOGRAPHER ACKNOWLEDGMENTS }

FOR MY WORK IN THIS BOOK, I give deep thanks to the triumvirate that was its immediate inspiration: Bunny Williams, Betsy Smith, and Margie Thorne. And for their longstanding inspiration, Beatrice Kernan and Delphine Eberhart. It has been an immense privilege to be invited to collaborate with Bunny, whose generous genius is matched by her kindness, wisdom, and humor.

I also thank Leslie Stoker for her belief in my work, as well as Dervla Kelly, Doug Turshen, David Huang, and Carolyn Coulter for their support. Appreciation for all, some of whose lovely homes appear in this book: my mother, Betty Short Fitterer, Eva Nies, Sally Cook, Kate White, Anne O'Malley, Liz Munson, Lucie Semler, Dottie Hayes, the Clements, Woody Counter, Suzanne Jones, Sandy Brooks, Belinda Rathbone, Tomie dePaola, Frank Eberhart, and Tucker.

*—Amy Archer*

Published in 2010 by Stewart, Tabori & Chang
An imprint of ABRAMS

Text copyright © 2010 Bunny Williams
Photography and place portraits copyright © 2010 Amy Archer

Library of Congress Cataloging-in-Publication Data

Williams, Bunny, 1944-
 Bunny Williams' scrapbook for living / Bunny Williams ; photography by
Amy Archer.
    p. cm.
  ISBN 978-1-58479-859-0 (alk. paper)
 1.  Interior decorating—Psychological aspects.  I. Archer, Amy. II. Title.
III. Title: Scrapbook for living.
 NK2113.W539 2010
 747—dc22
                                    2010018470


Editor: Dervla Kelly
Designer: Doug Turshen with David Huang
Production Manager: Tina Cameron


The text of this book was composed in Cochin, Didot, and Requiem.

Printed and bound in China
10 9 8 7 6 5 4 3 2 1

Stewart, Tabori & Chang books are available at special discounts when
purchased in quantity for premiums and promotions as well as fundraising or
educational use. Special editions can also be created to specification.
For details, contact specialsales@abramsbooks.com or the address below.

THE ART OF BOOKS SINCE 1949
115 West 18th Street
New York, NY 10011
www.abramsbooks.com